DETERMINED TO DREAM

Lessons I've Learned About Manifesting Vision
& Leaving a Legacy

Leah Jonet Albright-Byrd

Sharonda
Live your
beautiful legacy!

Leah
Jonet

This book is dedicated to every dreamer who has faced the powers of doubt, fear, and unbelief.

You are the dream.

ACKNOWLEDGEMENTS

There are many people that have encouraged me to write, too many to mention them all, but I'd like to thank every friend who believed in my dream even when I couldn't. You helped me live *my* legacy and conquer the lie that said that I couldn't. You now hold in your hands the fruit of the seeds you have sown. I'm forever grateful for your support!

To my pastors Scott and Karen Hagan, thank you for helping me heal and become a truer "Leah". Your care for me restored my hope in the power of spiritual leadership.

To Loren and Rachelle Ditmore, my brother and sister, thank you for being family, for not judging me when I fell apart, and for loving me relentlessly as God put me back together again. No matter where this life takes me, you'll always be my neighbors!

To my mother and my "Mommiesmoms", thank you for encouraging me to read. Reading at a college level in the 5th grade was possible because the two of you nurtured my love for literature and poetry. You gave me a gift that will last a lifetime. I also want to thank you for buying me reading lamps so that I didn't destroy my eyeballs (hehe)! Love you.

To my Dad, from blowing bubbles on my great-grandma's steps to long talks about any and everything, you are a gift from God and the only Dad I've got! Thank you for always reminding me that I'm loved.

To my Jesus, thank You for writing this book with me. You are the author, the greatest storyteller, and the best friend a girl could ask for. Thank You for waiting patiently for me to return to You and for loving all of Your prodigal sons and daughters so faithfully that the darkness will never win. I agape You.

TABLE OF CONTENTS

The room was still and I felt an indescribable peace that I hadn't felt in so long. Tears from a furious heart drenched my cheeks. David leaned forward and in a near whisper asked, "Do you know why that makes you angry?"

Could it be that this man had an answer that would destroy the lie?

Had I known the answer all along?

I sat up straight, wiped my face, lifted my head and looked him in the eyes to respond, "Why?"

Pointing his finger at me, he firmly declared, "Because you know that it's not true. So let this be your commissioning. It's time for you to go and do what you were created to do!"

INTRODUCTION
Dream Adviser

There are peculiar moments in life, where without warning, we find ourselves confronted by a Dream Adviser. That person may be male or female, they may be younger or older than you, or they may come from a background entirely different than your own. When you meet your Dream Adviser you will know, because the words they speak to you will pierce your heart, the air may suddenly become dense with anticipation *and* relief, and you will experience a profound conviction that your time has come. Suddenly, ignoring that "thing" that you've been dreaming of will no longer be an option, and the mere possibility of abandoning it will leave you unsettled.

Are you waiting for that moment to come?

Are you waiting for that Dream Adviser to come along who will help you muster the strength to stop *thinking* about your dream and actually *conceive* it? If you are, then I wrote this book for **you**.

On the other hand, maybe you're someone who doesn't believe that you have a "thing". Perhaps you feel stuck in a confusing time of uncertainty. I've come across many people who have somehow convinced themselves that they don't have BIG DREAMS. If that describes you, here's a vital fact you need to know:

People without big dreams do not exist!

There are those who wrestle with debilitating doubts and allow discouragement or "responsibilities" to delay the pursuit or diminish the powerful urge to see their deepest desires manifested. Just as there are those who are convinced that their dreams are insignificant (usually in comparison to the dreams of others).

Has doubt been distracting you?
Are you prone to comparison?

What is keeping you from manifesting your vision? Take a moment to pause, reflect, and be honest with yourself. As you ponder, I'm sure you can come up with an excuse that's pretty convincing, but I want you to answer these questions.

Have you ever been lied to?
Isn't it painful when you discover the truth?

The most daunting hurdle encountered on everyone's dream path is DECEPTION. Too many of us are convinced of lies about ourselves and our dreams, and as a result, we can't fully embrace the legacy we are intended to live. *That's* catastrophic.

Dream fulfillment is your birthright.

Another significant truth us dreamers must embrace is that a BIG dream is not about size; it's about significance. What are the things that are most significant to you that you have yet to attain? Those are *your* BIG dreams. You may not want to pursue what you've seen other dreamers go after, but your dreams are no less significant. Comparison is death to the joy we can experience when we manifest the vision we have in our hearts. Every dream you have is noteworthy (even the ones you've tried to ignore), but comparison, doubt, fear, and deception can become hope-draining traps. Thankfully, overcoming each of those obstacles is possible with the right kind of support.

There have been periods in my life where I aspired to change the world, and other times where I desired to simply change *my* world. In both seasons, I had an urgent need for a Dream Adviser, because dreams are meant to be manifested with the help of others. Your vision will require you to invite people to join you on your dream journey. Just make sure that the people you invite are Dream Advisers not Dream Destroyers or Dream Stealer but we'll talk more about that later.

Before we move on, it's important to point out that there's one more place people often get stuck on the dream journey, and that's in the land of in-between. When I started writing this book, I found myself in that place. A significant dream in my life had suddenly died (or so it seemed), and I was distraught. I suddenly went from being someone who was well-known for pursuing a BIG dream to being desperate for redirection and an infusion of hope so that I could dream again. I could not muster the strength alone. The inspiration for this book came at a time when I was searching frantically for books that could help me out of that in-between-place. At the pinnacle of my emergence into a new season of dream pursuits, I realized that instead of reading about someone else's experiences, I had to write about my own and thereby empower myself and others to move forward. As I began to think about my voyage and the voyages of other dreamers I've come to know over the years, I rediscovered the path to manifesting a vision; a narrow path that many dreamers avoid because of the requirements; a path that many before us have discovered and many after us will also travel.

It's the path of the dreamer.

Every human being has a legacy. You were created to make world-changing impact that outlives you and it's time to embark on the adventure that awaits everyone who chooses to be courageous and take BIG risks for BIG dreams. All the "what" and "how" questions can cause frustration. Even knowing the "what" of your dream journey can be annoying, if you don't know the "how". That's why I wrote *Determined to Dream*. This book is for anyone who is ready to advance; it's for the dreamer who needs an inspiring push forward from someone who has traveled this road and experienced success and failures. I want you to learn from my triumphs and pitfalls as you discover the true purpose for your dreams.

You are a dreamer with a LEGACY!

That's the universal good news for every dreamer. Legacy living is not reserved for the elite, the wealthy, or the naturally gifted. It is every human being's promise; it's a part of the human experience.

And there's more good news. This book won't consume much of your time. It's an easy to read, easy to digest guide that you can refer back to on your journey whenever you need encouragement to keep fighting. After Chapter One, each chapter will begin with a conversation where someone special advised me on my journey to manifesting vision and pushed me forward just as I'll be pushing you. I also want to urge you to answer the questions at the end of each chapter before you move on to the next one. The questions will challenge you to discover (or rediscover) your dreams, examine your beliefs, and conquer the pesky distractions that can became major obstacles if we allow them to. As your Dream Adviser, I want you to be valiant. It's time for you to live the life of a dreamer without regrets (even if you're in the land of in-between like I was).

VISION QUESTIONS

What are the biggest challenges for you when it comes to pursuing your dream(s)?

_____

_____

_____

_____

What's just one BIG dream you have had over the years that you've dismissed as either silly or impossible?
Remember, BIG dreams are not about size; they are about significance.

_____

_____

_____

Was it difficult to answer that question? If so, why?

_____

_____

_____

To get yourself moving forward, what do you think you'll need most? Courage, information, or hope? (It's possible to need all three.) Is there anything else do you need to get moving forward?

_____

_____

_____

What role (if any) has comparison, doubt, fear, and deception had in delaying your dream pursuits and plans?

_____

_____

"Of all the paths you take in life,
make sure a few of them are dirt."
John Muir

CHAPTER ONE
Cutting Class and Dirt Paths

I started cutting class in the 2nd grade. Most kids start cutting class in middle school or high school, and although I cut school at those ages as well, I guess I discovered my adventurous nature much earlier than most. When I was in elementary school, I lived in a small rural village in Germany known as Calden. As the only Black kid in town, I frequently struggled to stay focused amidst the daily challenges of racism and adapting to a culture so different than my hometown of San Francisco.

So...I began escaping.

It would start with an urge to leave class, then I would find the right time to sneak off to my bike and pedal as fast as I could until I was somewhere far enough away that no one could hear me sing my eight-year-old heart out. I had found my refuge; a place where I felt free to be myself and daydream about the future.

My school sat atop a hill and looked out onto a vast field that belonged to local farmers. Through the middle of the field was a long, winding dirt path. It led from one side of town to another, where there was nothing but forest.

My favorite part of that dirt path was a little run-down, one room house my mom and I called "Die Alte Hütte", which in English means "the old shack". It had an aged charcoal black potbelly stove in the corner, a tattered brown couch, broken windows, and newspaper scraps scattered across the floor that dated back to the early 1900s. It was freezing in the winter time and hot in the summer. Broken windows, a missing door, and mouse poop on the wooden slat floors made it evident that no one occupied it. Sometimes I'd play there and imagine it was my very own; that little house that sat between civilization and the wilderness.

As much as I loved the old shack, I was still terrified of the forest less than a mile from where it sat. Even when the sun shone brightly, my imagination, always vivid, told me that danger lurked beyond the boundary where the dirt path met the beginning of the woods. There may have been something beautiful out there, but I envisioned wild boars and the seven rabies shots right in my belly that my teacher swore I would need should I ever have been bitten by a rabid animal. The possibility of pain was enough to prevent my adventurous spirit from wondering into the mysterious.

The path of the dreamer is much like that dirt path in Germany. On your journey to your legacy, you will find yourself somewhere between your present life and the wilderness daydreaming about your dream, unaware of what awaits you in the dark forest (your future), and wrestling against the gravitational pull to your familiar surroundings (your comfort zone) because you aren't quite prepared to take the risk of traveling into the unknown.

Many dreamers look longingly towards the unfamiliar but feel trapped by the opinions of others, the inevitable fear and anxiety they will face or the challenges that lie ahead. Being uncertain about whether or not you have what it takes or wondering if your dream is even possible is a normal, albeit debilitating, part of the human experience. And just like little Leah, you will end up on the path to living your legacy primarily through the following three dream motivators:

1. a personal event (I was in a new country adapting to new culture)
2. a problem or a need (I was having trouble at school)
3. a direct sense of calling (I experienced the urge to go)

It's common for some of us to begin dreaming as children and then manifest our dreams as adults. Many of my daydreams out on that dirt path had to do with things I couldn't possibly have achieved as a child. I dreamt of a life much different than the one I was given. Day-to-day experiences were affecting my outlook and hopes for the future. Our perspective and priorities are shaped by our experiences. You may find yourself impacted by an event or series of events which deeply influence your take on what's most important in life. That's one of the best parts of life on this earth, no experience is wasted; even the ones that wound us deeply and seem to lack purpose.

"Life can only be understood when looking backwards but it must be lived forwards." – Soren Kierkegaard

At the beginning of this book, I included a conversation between myself and a man who helped me realize that I could no longer put off a particular dream. I *had* to see my dream come to life. Anger had risen in me because of a significant need I saw in my community that was unmet, a personal event that had forever changed my life, and a deep sense that *I* had to get involved in some way. These three dream motivators were blaring at me, compelling me to move forward. I want you to notice that I said that I was angry. When we think of dreams, we don't usually imagine them being attached to negative emotions. Most people try to suppress or avoid acknowledging the influence of anger in their dreams, but it's not as bad as it seems. When I was in college, I became a drug and alcohol counselor, and I taught anger management. It was often insightful to observe the way adults would discover that anger could actually be a motivator when it's channeled properly. When I began to daydream about solutions to the problem I saw, my anger was initially getting in the way of seeing clearly. As George Jean Nathan once said, "No man can think clearly when his fists are clenched." But once my Dream Adviser stepped in, I was able to appropriate my frustration and see the path that the problem created for me. I was able to channel my anger into passion.

If anger is motivating you, you will need to go through a process in order to channel it into passion.

When I was a kid, I visited that dirt path because of a problem. On *your* dream path, you may have faced problems that seemed insurmountable or you may have battle wounds from past wars you've fought and won in your personal or professional life that make you want to alleviate the pressure for other people who share your experiences. Those are both powerful aspects of motivation that can create significant momentum for you to launch forward, but anger and problems aren't the only propellers into a legacy life.

In his book *The Alchemist,* a fictional account of a young man pursuing a dream, author Paulo Coelho says that when we discover our personal legacy, the whole universe will conspire to help us achieve it. I'm always amazed to see the wisdom of that truth in my own journey and in the journey of others.

I'm reminded of one of my favorite artists who from the time he was a small child was drawn to music. Mali Music was classically trained at a young age and had his gifts cultivated by those around him who saw his potential. His family and those who saw his gift and passion supported him on his journey. He gradually developed his musical aptitude in ways that caused others to stand back and marvel—not to mention he has a distinct sound that is unmatched; a gift that influenced an entire generation and genre. He carved out his own path and fiercely dove into his music career. Years later, he has become a Grammy-nominated, internationally known artist. Now *that's* a dreamer!

But what about when you don't have a passion or talent that was cultivated from the time you were a child? That was my dilemma. Although I was definitely a dreamer, I was not drawn to a particular sport or instrument, and I did not have a passion for a certain career. After leaving Germany, a series of events led to some tragic experiences. I eventually dropped out of high school, and because I was unprepared for college, I didn't have aspirations to obtain a degree until later on. When I attempted to move beyond the in-between place where I was inspired to write this book, I came across a common question in the coaching and self-help realm: "What did you want to be when you were a child?" While that's a reasonable question, I was clueless and slightly discouraged because most of my childhood was about survival versus healthy development. Children should be encouraged to dream. But every dreamer's journey will be different. Sometimes you will be completely clueless. You may have come from a background where your dreams were not cultivated. Maybe you've known since you were a child who you want to be. Or perhaps you've discovered patterns of interest that you didn't realize were themes in your life. Maybe you've experienced significant pain that has shaped your dream. No matter how you've come to the dirt path (even if you got here by making horrible choices, as I often did), you will get to where you're going, if you're willing to be changed. Forever.

VISION QUESTIONS

Which of the three dream motivators has fueled your dream(s) either in the present or the past? Give an example.

_____

_____

_____

_____

What patterns/themes have been recurring in your life that are perhaps indicators of the kind of legacy you will leave behind? When your time on earth is done, what will people who know you well remember you for?

_____

_____

_____

_____

What problems or needs in society/culture have you seen that need solutions that you believe you can help with?

_____

_____

_____

_____

Are there any negative emotions (i.e. sadness, anger, guilt, anxiety) that rise to the surface whenever you think about your dream? If so, which one(s) and why?

_____

_____

_____

_____

FOREVER CHANGED...

"Are you sitting down?"

My heart instantly dropped, and the world seemed to revolve even slower on its axis. I paused for a moment and held my breath. I knew it had to be something serious, but considering I had just lost my aunt and my uncle in the last three months, I was not ready for another loss.

"What, Dad?"

"Leah... Bridget was killed!"

A million thoughts raced through my head, but only a few words managed to escape my mouth.

"NO, Dad, NO!"

Grief stabbed my heart as I dropped to my knees and began to sob violently in a corner of the hotel room. I could hear nothing yet everything. My little brothers stopped playing and looked at me, knowing something awful had happened. What we'd always been warned of had actually happened... to her.

My Dad's voice was full of sorrow as he said, "Someone strangled her to death. Her body was found on the 25th floor of the Mandalay Bay Casino. I'm so sorry this happened. You know she would've been twenty-two today."

CHAPTER TWO
Forever Changed

Running through the dark, screaming her name, I hoped she would hear me and come out of that man's house. She'd been in there far too long, and I just knew that something was wrong. She was only 14 and I only 15. When she finally came out, I was pissed. "Don't you ever do that again," I raged, as she hopped into my car. "I thought you were dead!"

I had no way of knowing that our scare that night was a prelude to an indescribably tragic loss. Dear, sweet Bridget Gray would lose her life only 8 years later. A sex-buyer murdered her; she became a victim to the awful realities of human trafficking. To make matters worse, I eventually had to fight through the shame and guilt that came with knowing that I introduced her to the sex-industry.

Losing Bridget was traumatizing. When it first happened, only a few people seemed to care and as the tabloids changed from "woman found slain" to "prostitute found slain", I watched in terror. Stigma and a lack of community education defamed the memory of a beautiful quirky girl whose life was stolen from her. The world didn't know her as "Bee Bee". They never got to see her dancing. They'd never laughed at her hilarious sense of humor or made up raps to her beat boxing. With one word the media had stripped Bridget Gray of her dignity. She was no "prostitute". She was a queen who never got to experience the freedom that I have known. Losing Bridget deeply affected my dreams and goals. I wanted her story to affect the world. People needed to know the truth; to see what I saw, to see every person who shared our experiences as a beautiful human being worthy of love, understanding, and an opportunity to heal. Bridget's death changed my life. When the opportunity emerged to tell others her story, I fought with all my might to help the world see that girls like she and I needed an army of community members to fight this atrocity. Becoming a voice for the voiceless became one of my BIG dreams.

Many of us want to leave an amazing legacy, but we must measure the cost that is always associated with dream pursuits. We must embrace the fact that our dreams will change us. In my case, I never would have chosen the loss of Bridget as a path towards manifesting a vision, but my legacy chose me! I was battling through my own painful healing process from child sexual exploitation, but the very moment that I discovered that Bridget was gone forever, I was changed forever. While grieving for what seemed like an unending time, my mother would watch helplessly as I lay on my bed curled in a fetal position, weeping inconsolably, with guilt and pain consuming my heart. There was no one around at the time that could understand the agony nor help me truly understand the victimization we'd both experienced. Later on that year, I transferred to a four-year university from the local city college and was required to declare my major. I went from being a girl who wanted to teach, speak, and potentially have a media career, to a woman who wanted to make Bridget's life count for something more than the awful news coverage the paper in Vegas had given her. So that fall, I chose to study psychology and theology to acquire the skill to integrate my faith with counseling practices. Finding specialized healing resources in the community I lived in was difficult as there weren't any services designed to address the extensive trauma of survivors of commercial sexual exploitation. The churches I attended offered much needed community but they too were unaware of how to support someone with our history. Bridget hadn't been able to find the intervention and support she needed in the foster care system either. Sadly, the systems we were in were unequipped to meet the overwhelming needs of a person who survived sex-trafficking. Over time, my determination to change that problem consumed my thoughts and plans for the future.

There are some of you reading this book that have lived through indescribable pain. As a person all too familiar with unbearable sorrow and loss, I applaud you for still being a dreamer. Even if you don't know what's next, the fact that you picked up this book means that you still have hope. I pray that my life and journey are a reminder that our pain doesn't have to deter us from manifesting great vision. Our pain can, in fact, shape our pursuits and passions. What better way to gain victory over our darkness than to shine brightly as overcomers who snatch other people right out of the grip of the same tragedies? Are you willing to be forever changed or are you going to allow your pain to deter you or convince you that your dream is impossible?

Now, let me add this caveat. If you are a person who has experienced any form of trauma and you want to help others, I ask that you first help yourself. Personally, I went through years of counseling before I started reaching back so that I could have a strong foundation, and even after doing so, fighting on the same battlefield that I had survived as a child was a great risk that cost me significantly. I don't say that to deter you but to protect you and share the wisdom that I received from my stepmother years ago when she encouraged me to get stable footing on the mountain I was climbing before reaching back for someone else whose foot was slipping. That does not mean you have to be perfect. I am, however, encouraging you to examine yourself, your healing needs, and the timing of a major dream pursuit (particularly when it directly relates to your own painful experiences). A counselor and/or trusted friends who understand your journey are great allies in helping you decide whether the time is now or you need a bit more room for healing. Honoring yourself and your healing journey is a part of the dream.

For those of you who are pursuing dreams that have nothing to do with tragic loss, I hope you are all the more inspired. If those whose dreams have been fueled by tremendous tragedy can find the bravery to move forward with their dreams, you should leave yourself no excuses. Let *this* be *your* "forever changed" moment. Make a declaration that from this point forward you will refuse to ignore your dream. Perhaps you want to start a tech company or maybe you want to go back to school. Do you have a flair for fashion design? Or an idea to start a nonprofit that will help your community? Have you always wanted to write a book but never truly allowed yourself to acknowledge and prepare for that dream?

Whatever your dream is, remember that if it is significant to you, it is significant. Period.

If after reading about my "forever changed" moment you still feel like you're lacking direction or are unclear about what your dreams are, I haven't forgotten you. Being unsure about what you want does not make you odd; it makes you human. So there's no need to panic. This is where it's time for you to get real. This is where you have to begin to tap into *your* desires and take caution not to shut down your ideas before you even begin exploring. The problems that most dream-doubters have are usually related to unbelief, past perceived failures, defeatism, comparison, or a lack of experience. Do not judge yourself if any or all of those internal obstacles are your struggle or if you happen to be a "late-bloomer" when it comes to dream pursuits. American culture has convinced us that we must achieve certain things by a certain time and if we haven't that we've somehow missed the boat. That's a lie. So climb right out of that box.

People have many reasons for thinking that they are "dreamless" or underestimating the significance of the dreams in their heart. Sometimes you just haven't encountered the "thing" that ignites you with passion yet or doubt has led you to dismiss the things that are significant to you. Or if you've already conquered a major dream in one season of your life you may be uncertain of what's next. Whatever the blockage is, it's time for you to choose. Will you dream (again) or will you ignore the desires of your heart? Don't be surprised if pessimistic thoughts rise to the surface when you answer the questions that follow. The lie always seems to become more convincing when we begin to uncover the truth.

VISION QUESTIONS

What experiences have "forever changed" you and how do they connect with your dreams for the future?

_____
_____
_____
_____

How have you prepared yourself to use those experiences to impact the lives of others (i.e. counseling, books, self-development classes, mentorship, etc.)?

_____
_____
_____
_____

If you knew you had no limitations to work on your dream, what would you immediately begin doing?

_____
_____
_____
_____

Dreams are things you think about but haven't committed yourself to yet. Name three small commitments you can make and complete in the next two weeks to work towards your dream.

_____
_____
_____
_____

I MUST...

"I have to take Thursday off for a biopsy I'm having done."

"Okay, but will you be here for the staff meeting?"

My boss seemed to be more interested in my ability to lead the staff meeting than my health. In my anger and frustration, I questioned the direction that my life was going. I knew that this wasn't my final stop, but what was I to do with a dream and no vision?

CHAPTER THREE
I Must

I was finally a manager. After working in support roles for years, I longed to have more influence and knew for some time that I possessed natural leadership abilities. Being in grad school full-time and obtaining a position as a Program Manager at a local nonprofit whose mission sort of aligned with my passions, was the logical next step in the direction of my dreams. But because I mainly saw it as a stepping stone, I had a hard time staying engaged a good majority of the time. My bent towards perfectionism and desire to gain experience with nonprofit management led to a determination to prove to my boss (and myself) that I was worth the $45k I would make working long hours at a place I didn't really want to be.

Now there are some that may say that because I'm a millennial, my thoughts about my place of employment merely demonstrated a lack of commitment and proper work ethic (insert smiley face here), but you know what? Though the generations who preceded millennials may pride themselves on working jobs they hate and/or are horribly bored with, all of the time they've given to someone else's dream may have very well kept them from the opportunity to pursue a dream of their own that could be both lucrative and satisfying with the right strategy and mentorship.

These are, of course, generalizations, but for some on either side of the generational gap, this rings quite true. Some of us millennials are too entitled and a bit lazy, and some baby boomers are stubborn and narrow-minded when it comes to learning from the younger generations. But hey… no judgment here. No matter which generation you represent, manifesting your vision and living your legacy will require you to make the internal shift from "I think I want to" to "I must."

Your dream may not require the same crazy leap that I eventually took, but it will most definitely require you to make some decisions that seem crazy to you and most likely to others. Being a dreamer will demand a bold march into the dark forest (especially during moments when your feet seem to be glued to the ground). Advancing from wishful thinking to action will almost always happen as a result of pressure.

The combination of inner and outer pressure was a strong motivator for me when I finally ventured into social entrepreneurship. My manager's display of insensitivity to my health issues and the work culture challenges I was facing were pressures that I initially alleviated by invoking as much change as I could in the role I occupied until I found myself constantly daydreaming about my dream. The pressure mounted internally to the point that I even considered moving to another state. There was this nagging "This ain't it" feeling that I could not dismiss, and I wanted something that I could not articulate.

What may have looked like discontentment and ungratefulness for the opportunities I already possessed was actually my emergence into the "I Must" phase of my dream. All I knew was that what I wanted was vastly different than what I was experiencing at the time. Bridget's Dream, the organization I longed to start in memory of Bridget, had been in the back of my mind for years, but I had no tangible action plan to move forward. So I did the best thing any dreamer can do.

I prayed.

Now, in a world where truth has become subjective and many people think of prayer as words spoken into the wind, I have to stop here and emphasize the role that prayer plays in the pursuit of dreams. I am a Kingdom Kid, so my full confidence (especially now) is in the power of God. Let me be clear, people who do not know Jesus *can* manifest vision. That is evident by the many incredibly talented people who do not believe in Christ. God is generous and has given *everyone* gifts. Yet, He is the Ultimate Creator. He created us all and when we come to know the One who gives us dreams, we become our truest selves. You were created in the Image of God and a life without knowing Him fuels a hunger that won't be satisfied by any other pursuit. It's like the child who is adopted by a loving family and given everything but can't quite fill the void of not knowing his biological family. To know God and be known by Him is the greatest gift we'll ever have access to in this dark world. Pursuing a dream is tantalizing! But it's no match for the joy that comes with knowing the Giver of dreams personally and intimately. Ultimately, our Creator is the inventor of creativity. He endows His children with the power to produce dreams so much greater than themselves. He shaped you (Psalm 139) so He knows best how you fit into this crazy beautiful world!

Take Billy Graham, one of the greatest visionaries and evangelists of our time, as an example. He reached 215 million people in LIVE audiences (without social media) in over 185 countries in his lifetime by taking an offensive message and sharing it in an enticing and non-threatening way. Even though the word "Gospel" means "good news," the true message of Christ is offensive to many people, especially in today's cultural climate, but armed with his dream (God's dream), Billy Graham was able to make history. This is just one of many examples of what God does in the life of someone who has given Him everything. Jesus said it best, "Anyone who intends to come with me has to let me lead. You're not in the driver's seat; I am. Don't run from suffering; embrace it. Follow me and I'll show you how. Self-help is no help at all. Self-sacrifice is the way, my way, to finding yourself, your true self. What kind of deal is it to get everything you want but lose yourself? What could you ever trade your soul for?" (Matthew 16:25-26, MSG). Jesus also said, "I came so they can have real and eternal life, more and better life than they ever dreamed of." (John 10:10, MSG).

So, needless to say, I decided to ask God for specific direction—the kind where doors of access to my dream would have to be blown wide open in either Sacramento or Atlanta. I started thinking that maybe, just maybe, my vision would manifest in another geographical location. In addition to the pressures that were mounting, I had a faith problem. Truthfully, although I am a believer,

I'd wrestled with doubting God's existence and involvement in my life like every human being does at some point or another, but there was no other source that promised me what the Bible promised. There was no one that could lead me the way I saw God leading people in the Bible or in the world around me. With this in mind, talking to God about my journey was imperative because I recognized my limitations. I had reached the limits of my human ability to discern what was in my best interest, and with what little faith I could muster, I began to try and move the mountain that was blocking me from my future. Looking back, I now know that there was no better way to approach my "I Must" season.

Literally a week after I prayed for doors to open in the city God wanted me in, I got a phone call and was asked to share my story with a group of teenagers who had just been released from Juvenile Hall in Sacramento. It was the first time, since my first media appearance in 2003, that I'd been given such a direct opportunity to reach people with my story. From that moment forward, I was caught up in a whirlwind of opportunity, and suddenly all of the pressure I'd been under started to make sense. God was pushing me into my legacy (but not without a little opposition).

The opposition you face will match your legacy!

For me, that meant I would be fighting a multi-billion dollar criminal industry as well as my own shame and pain. I was facing a GIANT with a slingshot and a rock. Before he became king, David faced the giant Goliath (who everyone feared). When I walked into the coffee shop the day that I was to share my story, I brought along a friend for support but I wasn't ready for what happened next.

When the girls I would be sharing with walked in, one of the women that was helping out with the group was my ex-boyfriend's ex-girlfriend. All I could think was, "There's no way I'm telling my business in front of this woman."

When you get to your "I MUST" season, you will be faced with an intense temptation to turn back. Your internal dialogue coupled with external challenges can make you question whether or not you are ready, but opportunity begets opposition, my friend. In those moments have a conversation with yourself and ask yourself how bad you really want your dream. No one else can live *your legacy,* and all the outside advice you can get will not help you *stay* in your "I MUST" place, until you learn to push *yourself* to keep your feet moving forward. I had to. In that moment I was either going to shrink back or hold my head high and do what I had come to do! I'm happy to report that I chose the path of the dreamer; even as my ego told me no, frustrations mounted, and my voice trembled as my heart raced, I chose courage in the face of fear.

That night I told my story backwards, beginning with who I'd become and ending with how I started. Each girl was sitting on the edge of her seat. Some cried and others sat there with blank stares. When I finished, one sat back in her seat, took a deep breath and said, "I just don't get it." "Don't get what?" I was curious to know what had her so perplexed. "I mean...I mean...you're just so...so *clean.*" My heart filled with joy because I knew what she meant. A person who survives the commercial sex-industry will often feel permanently flawed and dirty but that night her heart was filled with wonder and hope. "Well, sweetie, this is what Jesus does with a life that belongs to Him. He'll make you new!" I leaned back in my chair and smiled;

knowing that we all belonged there in that very moment, knowing that victory was ours no matter how dark the road had been.

Later on that week, I went to a spoken word event with my best friend. Halfway into the show, I turned around and could not believe my eyes. The first man to ever exploit me was standing at the bar with several women who I assumed were also being exploited. I turned to Kenya, told her who he was, and with my heart racing said, "I'm going over there to talk to him." She stared back at me in shock. When I approached him, he instantly recognized me, and I felt like I was in a time warp. It seemed that nothing in his life had changed. He shared that he'd just been released from prison on pimping charges, and I shared that I was going to start an organization for girls like me and Bridget. He was so caught off guard by my statement that he spit his drink out all over the bar. He laughed for a moment, and then with a serious tone said, "This is as close to love as these girls are going to get, and this is as close to love as I'm going to get." I took a deep breath, looked him in his eyes, and firmly yet tenderly said, "Now, you know *that's* a lie." To my surprise he agreed and diverted his eyes from my gaze. My heart was filled with concern and compassion instead of disdain (another indicator that I was ready to move forward with my dream). We exchanged a few more words, and I promised that I'd pray for him.

What a week! I'd come face-to-face with my past *and* my future, and I knew it was no coincidence because of the timing and the conversation I had with God just a week prior. From that distinguishing moment on, I was committed to my dream process. I began attending local congressional hearings about human trafficking and speaking at events, and I gradually found myself more and more distracted from my day job – distracted, anxious, excited, and fearful. It's common to experience a barrage of different thoughts and ideas about yourself and your dream when you're transitioning from dreaming to daring.

As you begin to transform during your "I Must" season, you will advance when you can do the following:

1. *accept that the internal and external pressures are designed to make you uncomfortable enough to take new risks,*

2. *embrace each thrilling new opportunity and understand that they come with opposition that may frustrate you and make you question yourself and your dream, and*

3. *finish your current season with patience, understanding that how you finish the last chapter will affect how you start your new chapter.*

It is important that you finish strong, because once you pursue your new dream, you will quickly discover the frustrations that come with needing other people's full investment. Even if your dream is to start a sole proprietorship or to do another form of independent work, you will likely rely on other people to help you enhance your dream. Giving your current season your very best effort will not always "feel" lucrative in the present moment (especially as the pressure increases), and it will not safeguard you from the apathy and unreliability you may face when others are helping you with your dream, but know this: the Golden Rule is timelessly true, no matter what you believe. "Do unto others as you would have them do unto you" (Luke 6:31). When your conscience is clear and you've given your best with pure intentions, not demanding a reward for every effort you've made but investing excellently, you'll gain rewards in unexpected ways when the time comes for *your* new dreams to flourish.

How will you respond to your "I Must" season?

Will you shrink back at the opposition or will you stay determined to dream even as fear starts to set in? Even as pressures mount? This is the season where you must examine your grit factor. Grit factor means "perseverance and passion for long-term goals coupled with a powerful motivation to achieve your objective." It is the measure of perseverance you possess to overcome obstacles that lie on your path. Grit has been seen as a virtue at least since the time of Aristotle. *Email me for a link to take a test that will help you determine your grit factor (leah@leahjonet.com).*

Through prayer, pondering, and planning, I eventually got to a point where the business plan for Bridget's Dream was developed, and a strategy for manifesting the vision was finally tangible. It took five years after Bridget's heartrending death to move forward into the "I Must" season, but once I got there, I was consumed by the vision and fell in love with my dream. You will fall in love with yours too.

VISION QUESTIONS

What pressures are you currently experiencing (internal/external) that could be indicators that you've entered your "I Must" season?

_____

_____

The difference between a dream and a vision is a plan. What steps do you need to take to develop a plan? What will it take for you to move from "I think I can" to "I must"?

_____

_____

_____

What are the obstacles that you foresee? How can you overcome them?

_____

_____

_____

What role will prayer, pondering, and planning have in this season of your life? Who makes up your squad of people who will not discourage your dream but help push you forward?

_____

_____

_____

Write out a vision statement. It should reflect your core beliefs and values and describe what your dream will look like when it's fully operative. Ready, set, go!

_____

_____

_____

HONEYMOONING...

"I don't know. I think we might have to quit our jobs," I said, as we sat at a coffee shop diligently working on some important tasks for the organization.

"I know, right? What are we gonna do?" My best friend Kenya was just as unsure as I was.

Shortly after our simultaneous epiphany, my phone began to ring. It was a local attorney I'd met a few months prior.

"When are you going to pursue this work full-time?" she blurted out, as soon as I answered.

I got up to walk out of the coffee shop to find a quiet place. It was as if this woman had overheard my conversation. "What are you afraid of Leah?" she asked.

"That God won't provide for me," I answered honestly. I could sense the weightiness of her question, and as I stood under the stars, it occurred to me that I was in an unexpected conversation with yet another Dream Adviser.

"Doesn't He provide for you now through your job?"

"Yes, but this is different." Surely she didn't think that getting a paycheck was the same thing as being on a God adventure and chasing your dream.

"Leah, it may seem like it is, but it's not! God provided you with the job you now have. You just feel more secure because you have a regular paycheck." Suddenly, I felt a rush of excitement and anxiety. Was it finally time to leave my comfort zone and wander into the wilderness?

CHAPTER FOUR
Honeymooning

There are three stages of intimacy. The first is infatuation, the second is wilderness, and the third is mature love. I learned this from one of my favorite professors in college, Dr. Bev Wiens. What I didn't realize at the time was that the stages of intimacy in relationships can also be applied to the pursuit of dreams.

When we hit our "I Must" season, we eventually enter into complete infatuation with our dream. We think of it constantly, imagine how amazing it will be, are filled with hope for future possibilities, and we start to spend a lot of time working on it. Without realizing it, you'll fall head over heels in love with your dream and transition into the honeymoon phase. This is where you will become desensitized to the great burden of responsibility you are taking on. It's a healthy stage you must go through so that you can begin to take the risks associated with your new dream. When you make a true commitment to your dream and you begin what I like to call "Honeymooning", you will start experiencing an indefinite period of joy and excitement; it's a beautiful, albeit temporary, season of infatuation.

When Bridget's Dream began, I was relentless in my pursuit of opportunities. The euphoria was unlike anything I'd experienced before and I knew in my soul that I was doing what I was called to do. Because we were meeting a need that was largely unmet in our region, the phone was ringing nonstop. I began taking media requests and was getting interviewed frequently. Becoming a spokesperson to spread the word about the cause as well as the organization was an unexpected joyful aspect of my role as Executive Director. There were clear indicators that it was time to invest myself wholly into my endeavor, so I quit my job and was offered a contract position that would allow me to continue to earn some income while building the nonprofit. It was an unanticipated source of provision and it afforded me the ability to pay bills and the time to focus on the mission.

All I could think about was the dream!

But that infatuation phase also included some discoveries that initially caught me off guard. When we fall in love, we know love won't be easy all the time, but we usually aren't ready for the sacrifices required of us. That's when reality starts to set in. With Bridget's Dream, reality gradually started to set in when I began to see that it was difficult to get people to give us money or to acquire the volunteer support of professionals who were skilled in building a nonprofit, *and* to add to the challenges, we suddenly hit a huge roadblock with acquiring our nonprofit status through the IRS. What could've taken six months ended up taking nearly two years, and it was beyond frustrating. But passion outweighed the problems.

The contract I'd been offered with my previous organization also came to an abrupt halt, so I suddenly found myself with *no* income. I was speaking frequently, but I didn't know how to turn my free gigs into paid ones. I was definitely on a huge learning curve and my commitment to following through on my pledge to my dream was suddenly being tested.

One day, as I vented my frustrations to one of my friends, he recommended I listen to a message called "Let the Vision Come from What God Has Taken You Through." That message gave me a fresh gust of energy and was just the reminder that I needed. While honeymooning, I began to learn that "every problem was an opportunity for [me] to discover creativity" (T.D. Jakes); hence, I learned to design websites, handle bookkeeping, manage volunteers, do media interviews (with some obnoxious journalists), create flyers, lead fundraiser events, and so much more. Even though I'd spent 10 years working for and volunteering with various nonprofits, it was quite different to lead one as founder and director. However, my infatuation with the dream helped me sustain momentum during early stages of development and the opposition that came with it.

When you're honeymooning, your love for the dream will surpass your small beginnings.

Money was the number one obstacle in my honeymoon phase. But when money was tight, there were people who unexpectedly invested in *me* and not just the dream. I had a friend who would literally give me 10% of her check every month, my stepfather gave me a loan (and eventually forgave my debt), and volunteers from my agency gave me food, paid my bills, and helped with gas. That was actually one of the best parts of honeymooning; I was united with other people who cared about me *and* my dream. There were people who would devote their time, energy, and skills to help. When we first started doing street outreach, for example, people would literally put their lives in jeopardy by going to dangerous parts of town to reach the girls and women who were victims of commercial sexual exploitation. Those volunteers *truly* cared, and that was not just a gift to the dream but a gift to my heart.

However, even with help from the community I became painfully aware of an old wound. One morning, as I sat with some friends over breakfast at my house, I vented about how I was having a hard time trusting people despite the fact that they were right there believing in the dream and helping me day by day. I'd learned very early on that needing others was dangerous, and that belief was deeply ingrained in my psyche (remember what I said about deception being the number one obstacle for dreamers). In my honeymoon phase I *had* to lean on others. It was probably one of the most difficult parts of my early journey, and just as a newlywed couple must learn to depend on one another in ways they never have before, you will have to learn to depend upon the people you meet on your journey.

I expected to be disappointed, and sometimes I was, but looking back I can clearly see now that the people who cared far outnumbered the people who didn't. Being joined by those who shared my passion turned out to be a redemptive experience that countered one of the most debilitating lies I ever believed. And that lie was that I was completely alone in the world. The honeymoon became one of the most beautiful times of my life. Once you make it to your honeymoon phase you will:

1.   Experience the bliss of infatuation with your dream.

2.   Discover that you can do much more than you initially thought you could.

3.   Receive encouragement from people who believe in you and your dream.

4.   Begin to learn that you're not as trusting or confident as you thought that you were. That's okay and perfectly normal!

5.   Face discouragement from people who do not understand.

Manifesting your vision and leaving your legacy will almost always make certain people uncomfortable.

Crying about a lack of financial resources became a consistent part of my journey. One day I shared those fears about bills and my credit with my mother. She responded by saying, "Well, when you get a job..." Now, because I was still wrestling with my own self-doubts and a deep sense of inadequacy, I heard her comment as a criticism and assumed it meant that she didn't take what I was doing seriously. That's why it's important that you're not caught off guard if some of the people closest to you do not initially understand your dream or the choices you make on your journey or possibly even become obstacles on your path. Do not focus your energy on proving them wrong. I repeat, do NOT focus on proving the validity of your dream to anyone. I, sadly, did not respond to my mother with love or an understanding of her point of view and concerns. My initial response was to get angry and withdraw without realizing that doing so was a reflection of a significant area of needed growth in *my* life, not hers. During your honeymoon phase you will begin the process of coming face-to-face with *you*. The good and bad news is that the honeymoon phase is designed to come to an end. Before I even knew what was happening, I found myself traveling down an unexpected road.

VISION QUESTIONS

Which aspects of manifesting your vision bring you the most joy and excitement?

_____

_____

What skills and abilities do you already possess that will help you launch forward and save you money?

_____

_____

Who are your Dream Advisers, and how can you get them more involved during your honeymoon phase? You will need all the support you can get. Don't be afraid to ASK!

_____

_____

Who are the people who you foresee will be dream-doubters or dream-stealers, and how can you protect your vision from them without allowing yourself to become offended or discouraged by them?

_____

_____

AM I CRAZY...

"Leah, BET just called for you!" shrieked Amanda, my right hand girl; the Robin to my Batman.

"Wait… wait a second. Did you just say BET?" There was no way that that THE Black Entertainment Television I had grown up watching as a child was actually calling to ask ME to be on their network? "OH MY GOD! What's the number? I'll call right away!"

Quickly taking the number down, I ran out of the store, my heart pounding.

This was a destiny moment like none I'd ever experienced before. My excitement was coupled with an incredible sense of relief, as in that moment, somehow the challenges I had been facing seemed less significant.

CHAPTER FIVE
Am I Crazy?

Statewide committees, national and international news appearances, filming for documentaries, speaking engagements at conferences all over the country, full-time CEO work (overseeing every aspect of funding, development, and programming), policy work, and advocacy efforts filled my calendar.

My dream was in full effect.

From developing a business plan at a table at a coffee shop with my best friend to interviews on Katie Couric's talk show and BET; it was unbelievable! My dream manifested into a vision that was growing quickly. Hundreds of children, women, and families were being reached through Bridget's Dream, and millions of Americans were learning about one of the most significant civil rights issues of our time.

The night of Obama's re-election, we were all pacing anxiously as we ate hors d'oeuvres and waited on the results of both the presidential election and the vote for Proposition 35, the Californians Against Sexual Exploitation (CASE) Act. Would Obama be reelected? Would the proposition pass?

Not only did Proposition 35 pass, but it made state history with the highest amount of voter support EVER. When we got the news, one of my sheros (Daphne Phung, founder of California Against Slavery) grabbed me and hugged me, tears streaming down her pretty face. We cried, laughed, and were overcome with indescribable joy. Never had I felt such victory. Nearly 100,000 law enforcement officers in our state would receive human trafficking training, and the criminal penalties were going to be increased for traffickers. It was a BIG dream fulfilled! I began to believe in the power of the vote for the first time in my life, and I was *deeply* impacted by the fact that people *actually* cared.

I could still remember the day, ten years prior, when an older lady at my church asked me, "So, baby, did you just like sex?" I could still remember the title of the Oprah Winfrey show I was on in 2003: *Teenage Suburban Prostitution – Shocking America.* I could still remember my boss's cold response when she found out that Bridget had been killed. *"Was she a hooker?"*

The SHAME of it all…and the pain was still fresh in my memory yet the world was evolving to finally recognize that children were not "prostitutes" they were victims of human trafficking.

My heart was filled with joy at the realization that I was no longer the girl that feared people's judgment about my past; I was a woman with influence.

I was living my dream and leaving a legacy!

When you manifest your vision, you can change the world. Forever.

Whether you change one life or one million lives, making the choice to manifest your vision is a world-changing voyage. I was nearly speechless that evening as I stood on stage and sang "Great Is Thy Faithfulness". I still can't believe I sang on stage, but when you are living in the manifestation of a dream that's been in your heart for a long time, it will produce boldness, and my boldness to sing on stage that night was a reflection of how triumphant I felt. There aren't too many experiences in life that will exceed those moments when you realize that you're living in the fulfillment of your deepest desire and that your dream was possible.

Bridget's story had been spread across the state and beyond. Her death had not been in vain. I was determined to dream despite the hopelessness I had once battled and the despair that had consumed my life when Bridget was killed.

When I first met the Dream Adviser who God used to commission me in the conversation I shared at the start of this book, I wasn't just angry because of the injustice of losing Bridget, but I was raging angry with God. Losing her fractured my relationship with Him. I'd hoped and prayed that she would be free from prostitution, but she did not have the support she needed because there were no services and no one identified her as a victim of a crime committed against her (not by her). So you can imagine how crushed and hurt I was that God would *allow* this dark tragedy to happen. Honestly, my anger towards God was even greater than my anger at the man who killed her. I needed to see victory just as much as the girls that I was fighting for.

That night God gave us victory!

I drove home that evening down the same road Bridget and I had traveled on a dreadful night back in 1999 when I asked her, "Are you sure you want to do this? Because once you do, your life will never be the same." She wasn't old enough to know what I was asking her and I wasn't old enough to understand what was happening to either of us. It wasn't a choice to be exploited. She was forced into the sex industry just as I had been. But *this* night, November of 2012, was different. It had brought redemption. Even though Bridget was long gone, I felt so much joy at the thought that I'd been able to take her story so far. Yet, as a one hour drive turned into two hours, it wasn't long before thoughts about all that had transpired within the week prior to that night started to flood my mind. Five days earlier, I had been standing in a courtroom hearing for my little brother, who was facing 12 years in prison. The day after that, my god-brother had committed suicide. Both of them were only 19 years old.

When I finally got home that night, I was filled with a mixture of joy and sadness. I sat in my driveway for a while pondering everything and then slowly walked to the front door. When I stepped into the house, it had to be fifty degrees or less in there, and as I went to flip the light switch, I discovered that my lights were off. I started to get angry but calmed myself, lit some candles, and decided to deal with the issue in the morning. I knew why the lights were off. The bill hadn't been paid in several months.

It was pouring rain when I woke up the next morning, and the weather matched the heaviness in my heart. It was almost like the elation from the previous night's victory had dissipated, and I was back to reality. That day I made my way down to the welfare office, where I would apply for food-stamps. I hated the fact that I was working incredibly hard, yet struggling to take care of simple things like food and electricity bills.

It was difficult to muster the internal strength to face so many obstacles, knowing full well that my team was relying on me for direction and encouragement. A ton of bricks was on my chest and my arms and legs were heavy as I fought back tears, anger, and anxiety the entire day. I had already known what it was like to be stripped of everything (including my dignity and my humanity). Hadn't I already paid my dues? So when I looked around the welfare office, I thought to myself, "I don't belong here." Partially because I was judging the people I was looking at (sadly but honestly), partially because my mother had once been on welfare, leaving me stained by the memory of the shame that came with paying by food stamps (that was before the state issued debit cards), and partially because I just felt like I deserved better.

Hours passed by as I sat there waiting and hoping that someone would hurry up and call my number. That's when my phone rang, and a volunteer from Bridget's Dream asked where we were having our meeting that evening. I told her it would be at a coffee shop, and when she asked why we weren't meeting at my house, I gave her the truth. "It's because the lights are off." She then shared that she was already planning to give me $50 to help me and that she would bring it by my house. You'd think that would've comforted me some, but I was so angry I couldn't even feel gratitude. I forced a "thank you" and quickly got off of the phone.

It was getting close to the time that the welfare office was supposed to close, and I ached to get out of there. Suddenly a message came blaring out of the overhead speakers: "Our computers are down. I repeat, our computers have just shut down. We are experiencing technological problems and will not be able to process any more paperwork today." My head was going to explode. Was this a cruel joke?

I hopped in my car, full of rage, and drove home trying not to cuss and scream at God. My electricity bill was $214 dollars. I had $14 in my bank account. What good was an extra $50 going to do me? I pulled up in front of my house, parked, and dragged myself to the mailbox where Cathy, the faithful volunteer, had left me a gift. I had expected to open the envelope and find $50, but to my disbelief, I found $200. It was the exact amount that I needed in order to pay my bill. Cathy had no clue she had filled my need so perfectly. Hot tears streamed down my face and embarrassment filled my heart. I felt foolish for not trusting that God would provide for me. Doubt, fear, and unbelief had so effected my mood and disposition that I was rendered incapable of trusting. When I saw the need had been met, I promptly went and deposited the money and paid my utility bill. I wish I could say that such an obvious provision of my needs obliterated my doubt in God's care and concern for me and my dream, but it didn't. A way had been made but anxiety was still my constant companion.

That season of my journey was the best and the worst. Coming face-to-face with the mountains and valleys of my vision while celebrating monumental achievements and facing a flurry of challenges was bringing out the best and the worst in me. There were even days when I didn't even want to get out of bed. I was battling a depression that I couldn't seem to get anyone to understand. Gradually, I discovered that there were a lot of people who shared my history who were also leaders like me who were having a hard time dealing with the pressures and demands. I simply wasn't coping well. It eventually got to the point where I began questioning myself again, just as I had done during the honeymoon phase. The pressures were mounting, and I felt utterly crazy. Had I misread what God was doing? Was I even supposed to start this stupid organization? Why weren't things coming together?

Building the board was another daunting task of nonprofit development that I seemed to be ill-equipped for, I faced unbelievable amounts of anxiety nearly every time we went and did street outreach, the phones would not stop ringing with people in need, and my whole team had to be trained from the ground up. There were literally no people in my region that had enough experience with the population we were serving, so I found myself constantly educating people. What started off as elation and an opportunity to make a difference was slowly becoming a nightmare.

Sure, I had loved being able to be on the BET stage and educate the world about domestic human trafficking alongside the Boko Haram tragedy, where 276 Nigerian girls were kidnapped and trafficked. I also loved the look of relief when parents realized that they would not have to go through their child's exploitation alone. I thanked God for the moments when the Bridget's Dream team had helped reunite girls with their parents, and I rejoiced when Prop 35 passed and changed California forever.

It was a dream come true.

It was *my* dream. Wasn't it?

I mean, I'd dreamt of making a difference since college. Since before I had even graduated, I knew that I absolutely had to make a difference. And now, here I was battling anxiety every day, broke, unable to pay my student loans, unable to develop a steady funding stream for the organization, and unable to relax. Without realizing it, I'd hit the "Am I Crazy" stage of dream pursuits.

When you are in full motion of manifesting your vision that is when the most opposition can arise.

This season is where the authenticity of your vision is tested, and it is also where *you* will be tested. I thought that I really trusted God when I set out to venture into the unknown, but what I discovered was a vast well of unbelief. Pride and temper tantrums became daily struggles as fear, anger, resentment, and jealousy surfaced.

When you hit your "Am I Crazy?" phase, you will:

1.   *experience incredible victories and get a taste of the fulfillment you've been seeking*

2.   *learn more about yourself (the good, the bad, the ugly)*

3.	*run into unanticipated, seemingly insurmountable obstacles, battle intense discouragement, AND*

4.	*question everything you thought you knew about your dream, yourself, and God.*

This is when you start to discover the deepest truth about a legacy life. You see, this dream journey will require everything you have and even some things you don't have. It will force you to know yourself and God more intimately. Manifesting a vision and living a big dream is not for the faint of heart. You will have to fight many battles that you feel unequipped for. That's why many people never even make it to the "Am I Crazy" phase. But let me just put your mind at ease. If you make it to this phase, you *are* crazy! You have to be a little crazy to do crazy, amazing things.

The goal of this phase is for you to be completely transformed into an unrecognizable you.

VISION QUESTIONS

What are some of the skills and abilities required for your dream that you don't possess? Who do you know that has abilities in those areas and could be willing to help you?

_____

_____

_____

What are some of the ways that you've gotten discouraged during past dream pursuits? How did you respond? What can you do differently?

_____

_____

_____

How will you celebrate your victories? Name 3 rewards you plan to give yourself when you have manifested your vision.

_____

_____

How will being transformed into an "unrecognizable you" be helpful for you in this season? How will it affect your perspective of yourself?

_____

_____

_____

What will you do to keep a healthy balance with all of your responsibilities, need for rest and relaxation, and the demands of your dream pursuit?

_____

_____

UNRECOGNIZABLE YOU...

"What's the most important thing in your life right now?"

My colleague had set up a meeting between myself and a guy that she said was an excellent coach. I'd spent my weekend with her at a winery crying my eyes out, so she suggested that I spend some time with this guy. But as soon as I sat across from him at Panera Bread, and he began to interrogate me about my life, I started second-guessing my decision to meet with him.

"Well, the most important thing in my life right now is the organization that I run!" I answered somewhat confidently.

"What does it give you?" he asked.

I hesitated. "Purpose."

He smiled, and with his thick South African accent said, "So if I take it away, you have no purpose? The idea that your purpose exists in this thing is funny to me."

What did that mean? Of course this was my purpose, though I did have to admit that things weren't going the way I'd anticipated that they would. "Well, right now I'm running myself ragged with it since I have no parameters."

He smiled again, "Do you want me to hurt your feelings?"

Oh God, here it comes!

"Leah, you're not going to win the fight! What you are doing is absolutely noble and has great societal and social value, but because your self-value is undiscovered,

it puts you in a very vulnerable position and causes you to operate out of fear. What we're doing is working towards the story of YOU, even though your mind wants to shut me out. All that you know how to do is fight, and though it may appear to onlookers that you are fighting for everyone else, what we're really fighting for is for you.

You want to know how the unworthiness keeps surfacing? Well, the more you fight, the more the lights come on to showcase your life. Then you do the rest; you do the self-mutilation worse than any trafficker could ever do. In fact, you're so good at it, that it takes nothing for you to go there in a heartbeat, and it shows up in the behaviors that were there even before you left your parents' house.

Just be willing to see! There's a dominant pattern in your mind that's making you jump from thing to thing. It may seem useful because you are able to get a lot done, but when your mind jumps from thing to thing, it's really because it doesn't want to be present where it is. All of this stuff is covering something you're unwilling to see. Are you willing to see this thing for what it is? Do it without judging yourself. I can be a doorkeeper to open the doors where you need to see. Where do you want to begin? Because an explosion is going to come."

How could this man, in a matter of moments, know me and see me more clearly than I could see myself? "I want to see it all," I said. "I don't want this to run my life. I'm always obsessing over certain things, and I don't tell most people about it, but the truth is that I don't feel adequate."

He sighed and leaned back in his chair. "Now we're getting somewhere. Inadequacy is a transportation *system from the past. It all points to self-value. When inadequacy surfaces, you end up doing something to suppress it. Leah, you genuinely believe you are inadequate, and you are also untrusting. You're sitting there thinking, 'Who the f*** does this guy think he is?' The whole time you've been here you have not relaxed once. But I'm speaking to the part of you that lives in a different space, a hidden space.*

This will only hit you a few days from now, which is why you need to record this, but you need to get past the resistance. It has one purpose only: to keep the status quo in place. It is worse than any human being you know, because it will use you as leverage just to stay in place. It will even control your behavior, because you've surrendered all of your power to it. You'll only get to heartbreak and destruction this way.

You're a pretty girl that everyone wants to come close to, but once they get too close, you run because YOU decide the terms. And that's why you always feel unloved, Leah. Now you must recognize your resistance pattern, though fear and self-judgment won't allow it because they own you. The work that you do gives you an outlet to prove to the world that you are a worthwhile human being. And that's perfectly okay, because once you see the truth you will discover who you really are! Sure, you're great at what you do. That's the power of having lived through something; you can bring love to a specific dark space that other people can't. But you don't want to be in this prison anymore. You own the key and the responsibility to start doing things differently, but you have to start going to places that up until now have been off limits; the place where all the pain lives."

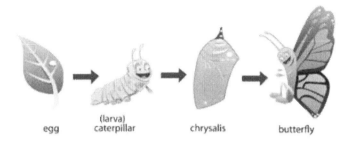

egg   (larva) caterpillar   chrysalis   butterfly

CHAPTER SIX
Unrecognizable You

My life hurt.

How in the world did I go from being excited about my dream to feeling like I was living in a nightmare? When I was younger, my "Mommiesmoms" (my grandmother) told me that she hated Sundays. I would always wonder why, until I started hating Sundays too. Sundays were the days when my whole world slowed down. I wasn't Leah the CEO, Leah the activist, or even Leah the survivor; I was just Leah. Those mornings I would go to church, listen to a sermon, and then dread going home. My home was no longer my sanctuary. I hated being there, because that's when I would hear "me" the loudest.

All week long I could stay busy, travel, speak, and change the world, but the reality was that *my* world was crumbling. Mostly everyone saw me as a competent, confident leader, but when I looked in the mirror, I saw struggle and stress. My cycle became work hard, go home, overeat, cry, and stay up late, only to do it all over again the next day. But on Sundays, I just had to BE. I'd walk into my house, lay on the couch with my cats, and an old familiar visitor would come my way with the most oppressive accusations he could find. The antagonist, the enemy of my soul, was at it again. I'd always been a threat to the kingdom of darkness and he was determined to beat me down any way possible.

TJ, the coach who had confronted me, was right! I was in a nonstop battle with fear and judgment. They were two familiar tools the enemy liked to use against me. The thoughts that seeped into my mind would weigh so heavily on me that I felt like I couldn't get off of my couch. So I ate and ate, feeling more and more defeated. Wishing that things were different, I became jealous of other leaders and organizations that seemed to be thriving, and though I longed for more than what I was experiencing, I felt hopelessly stuck in a workaholic cycle set on self-destruct.

That lasted for four years. Four years of running myself ragged. Four years of fighting hard. That was, after all, what I knew to do best. Running and fighting were two responses to life I'd learned early on. Running away from home at the age of 14, fighting through every season of pain I'd faced, and becoming a fighter for others who'd faced similar tragedies was suddenly all catching up to me. It was time to face the fact that I was still running and fighting. But for what? My fuse was short, and I was easily irritated and frequently discouraged. No matter what I did, I couldn't seem to move beyond where I was. "Where is God? Where are the answers to my prayers? Where are the miracles?" I said one day, as I pounded my fist on the table while talking to my big brother Loren, who was a longtime friend. He looked at me in that special way only a big brother can, and firmly said, "You wanna see a miracle? *Get up* and go look in the mirror!"

His words hit me hard. Hesitantly, I got up from the table, and went and looked at myself in the mirror. I didn't recognize myself. What happened to the dreamer who had started this journey? The person who stared back at me that day was different. My eyes were darker, my disposition was confused and distraught, and my mindset was cynical and doubtful. Even though my brother was right, I couldn't find the hope and faith that I needed to move beyond where I was. I was resentful. How could I stand on stages, help other people build their organizations, change laws, help survivors and their families, overcome my own victimization, and *still* not build the organization that I had dreamed of building? What good was I, if I couldn't live my dream?

Or wait... wasn't I already living it?

I had experienced some unbelievable feats. The scope of my contributions to the human trafficking movement in my region and beyond was vast. Even so, I couldn't *feel* the success for some reason. I couldn't acknowledge that anything I'd done was actually "good enough." And why was I unrecognizable? Well, friend, it's because I'm a dreamer.

We are designed to dream dreams that not only change the world but also result in a radical change within us.

My world had been completely turned upside down. Facing myself and the reality of the bitterness, resentment, jealousy, depression and hopelessness I was experiencing was beyond painful. I had even returned to smoking marijuana in an attempt to relieve my stress after

13 years of not smoking the drug that had led me to other drugs as a teenager. I was in an affair and then an abusive relationship right after that. My inner life was in turmoil. And as painful as it was, I'd finally reached the place where God had wanted me to be all along.

See, when you tell God "yes" and choose to follow HIM on a journey towards manifesting a dream, *you* will grow, and you will discover parts of yourself that you would rather not. Not so that you can recoil with shame and self-deprecation. There's no room for those destructive emotions in the life we've been given. Instead, you must learn to embrace that it is the manifestation of your vision that will bring out the truest version of you. In the end, this process won't just be about your vision. It will be about being refined. You are more important to God than your dream, and until you are able to see yourself as God sees you and see Him for who He is, your dream (and anything else you place your hope in for that matter) will be a poor substitute for the joy and love found in Him alone. Your dream can't give you the abundant life because Jesus is the source of life. He is the way!

As you pursue your dream, you will travel down the path we all must travel. At risk of using an overused metaphor, I have to point out the lifecycle of the butterfly. There's much about this beautiful critter you probably don't know. While going through my painful time of transformation and transition, I was sitting at a coffee shop in the middle of nowhere. Okay, I was in East Texas. Not exactly the middle of nowhere, but for a city girl it was pretty secluded. It was a totally different environment, the perfect atmosphere for a cocoon. Let me explain. The butterfly lifecycle occurs in 4 stages:

1. **Birth** – 5 days – quick stage

2. **Caterpillar** – the eating and growing stage. In this stage the caterpillar grows really fast because it eats a lot, becomes too big for its skin, and sheds up to four times in a process called molting. To molt is to cast off and to throw off the old layer. In this stage the focus is consumption and growth.

3. **Chrysalis** – when the caterpillar is done growing, it becomes a pupa. The pupa matches its surroundings and is hidden so that others cannot see it, this protects it and keeps it from getting hurt. This is the resting and changing stage. Here is when it starts to turn into a butterfly and begins to look completely different than it did before (unrecognizable you).

4. **Imago** – the chrysalis opens and the butterfly emerges, this is when it becomes an adult, a beautiful imago. When the butterfly emerges its wings are damp, soft and folded against its body, tiny and shriveled. The butterfly is also very tired. So the butterfly rests. Once rested, the butterfly will be ready to start flying, blood starts to pump into its wings, to get the wings working and flapping, after this it can learn to fly. Surprisingly, butterflies cannot fly very well at first. They need a lot of practice but it doesn't take them long to learn.

There's more: *Butterflies need the sun to fly. A butterfly's first job is to make sure that its proboscis works (its mouth) so that it can drink. Butterflies are nearsighted, they can only see about 10-12 feet in front of them and they can only see by following the ultraviolet markings produced by the sun.*

There's so much to consider here. First let me reiterate; I am a creationist. In other words, I believe God made the earth and everything in it. When we look closely, there are many beautiful ways that the creation points to the Creator. When I researched the butterfly it became such an unexpected source of revelation. Its evolution parallels our dream journey and growth as His peculiar creation. As the butterfly needs the sun to fly, we need the Son rise above the challenges of living and to reach the heights He intends for us to reach. As the butterfly can only travel 10-12 feet at a time because it can only see with the sun's light, we too must rely on the Son's light to guide us and He does so one step at a time. His word is a lamp to our feet and a light to our path (Psalm 119:105). We are come alive and defeat stressful thought patterns when we learn to truly trust Him for everything. It is completely possible to live a life of rest in Him! Our goal is to transition from each season of dreaming into an unrecognizable version of ourselves.

In our caterpillar phase we grow and grow consuming information through experiences (both the good and bad). We shed layers of lies we've believed and versions of ourselves that are dated. Where we differ from the butterfly is in our longevity. As human beings we cycle through many phases of life until our life as we know it on this earth comes to an end. We will cycle through our butterfly experiences many times, reaching higher heights and new pinnacles, seeing all that God wants us to see with the time He's determined for us. In my most recent caterpillar phase I shed many layers while discovering the essence of Leah. Beyond my traumatic experiences and the desire to change the world for those who shared them, was a woman with dreams and passions that had nothing to do with pain. When the time came to evolve, I began to change because of the "yes" deeply embedded in my soul. My determination to follow the best path resulted in my surrender to the customized process that helped me to evolve. Transparent moment: I honestly wouldn't have chosen my transformation process if I was left to my own understanding. The surrendered life is incredibly beautiful *and* incredibly difficult. But the only way to the legacy God intended for you will always include humility and absolute surrender. We need not fear Him. Respect Him and honor Him? Absolutely. But fear Him and His plan for us, never. He's the best Father and Friend there is.

A legacy life is a life that willingly travels a narrow path in order to achieve the greatest victory. "Enter through the narrow gate, for wide is the gate and broad is the road that leads to destruction, and many enter through it. But small is the gate and narrow the road that leads to life, and only a few find it" (Matthew 7:13-14 NIV). A legacy life is a life that faces painful disappointments and obstacles that seem to be unending, but does not give up. It embraces dreams, even in moments when they seem more like nightmares. And it chooses to walk the narrow path that leads to His heart. You have the kind of life that Jesus died for so that you can experience what it really means to be a dreamer of *His* dreams.

VISION QUESTIONS

What about my conversation with TJ resonated with you? Who do you have in your life to confront you and help you get back on track when you start having challenges while you pursue your dream?

_____

_____

How will you deal with the battle against fear and self-judgment? What are the tactics that the enemy uses against you as he tries to fight you for your dream?

_____

_____

_____

Where are you in the butterfly lifecycle? Men, I know it may be challenging to envision yourself as a butterfly but go with me on this one. ☺

_____

_____

_____

If Jesus were to have a conversation with you about your journey right now, what questions would you have for Him?

_____

_____

_____

What are you allowing to stop you from giving God your complete "YES?"

_____

_____

DO DREAMS DIE?

"What do you need to hear from Bridget?"

I sat on my counselor's couch weeping. I had come to process a work issue, but now I felt like I was being gutted.

When my counselor asked me that question, I didn't know what to expect. I thought for a few moments, and what rose to the surface made me take a deep breath.

"That it's okay for me to let go!"

That's what Bridget would have said to me if she were there in that moment. She would have wanted me to move on with my life at some point. She would've wanted me to LIVE.

CHAPTER SEVEN
Do Dreams Die?

I was intrigued from the moment we had our first conversation.

"Where do you see yourself in the next six months?" he asked.

"Bridget's Dream is going to…"

I couldn't even finish my statement before he said, "I didn't ask you about Bridget's Dream. I asked where you saw *yourself* in six months."

There was no answer to the question. Somehow I'd become my organization and couldn't separate myself from it. My identity was fully wrapped up in Bridget's Dream. While driving down a main street in Sacramento that morning, March 2nd, 2015, the man that I would spend the next year of my life dating asked me a question that made me see that I had somehow gotten lost in my dream. I had been so consumed with Bridget's Dream that I did not know what I wanted for *myself* anymore.

Those first few months of 2015 were intense. The day-to-day tasks of running the organization were overwhelming, and subsequently, I began to grow weary of all the constant requests for media appearances and speaking. Eventually I began to hate the human trafficking movement. Competition amongst survivor leaders, competition amongst nonprofit leaders, the frustration of tokenism, and repeatedly going back into the darkest memories of my life, running Bridget's Dream and the nonstop needs of our girls were all driving me crazy. My body and mind were beyond burnt out and a familiar dullness and numbness swept over me. There was no color in my life; everything turned gray and I was barely surviving instead of thriving.

The conversation I had at the start of this chapter was with my therapist and it left my heart deeply disturbed. Going to see her to vent about some work related issue turned out to be life-transforming. I knew from my training and years in the mental health field that keeping a therapist on deck would be imperative for me while fighting human trafficking but I was unprepared for the insight I received. My counselor unexpectedly became my Dream Adviser in the conversation I shared before this chapter began. After that unforgettable session I walked away with a nagging question: was it time for me to quit my own organization? Was Bridget's Dream going to die? I couldn't wrap my mind around the agonizing thought. But without my permission a light bulb clicked on.

Once Truth bursts forth it cannot be silenced.

Bridget would *not* have wanted me to kill myself while running the organization. She would have wanted me to live my life to the fullest. She would've wanted me to honor and pursue ALL of my dreams. Especially my dream of freedom from the thoughts and emotions that I'd been at war with for many years. The same battles I'd seen so many others fight; the battle I'd seen that had overtaken some of the people I'd grown up with.

Around that time was when I'd made the decision to start smoking weed again to self-medicate. I sat one day with my mother, high and in tears. "How am I supposed to show these girls freedom when I don't feel *completely* free?" I asked. Five years of counseling, developing a national platform, and all the other efforts I'd made to achieve a sense of wholeness almost seemed futile in that moment. The deep sense of worthlessness that I had been running from when I left home in 1998 was blaring at me in my 30s. I felt insufficient, unloved, and unfulfilled. I still hated parts of me and somehow the teachings on "identity in Christ" in the churches I'd attended hadn't penetrated past some significant layers of pain in my heart. Sure, I didn't start Bridget's Dream with some conscious awareness of my need to feel worthwhile, but perfectionism, fear, self-judgment, and obsession with the organization were all indicators that something was wrong. Something needed to die.

I've heard it said that God and the devil are after the same thing. They both want to kill you. Sounds crazy? Well, I believe that it's true, except the devil wants to steal from you, kill you, and destroy your life. God, on the other hand, wants you to die to *yourself* and a life of self-sufficiency apart from Him so that you can experience *true life*. There's a difference. A huge difference.

That period of transformation certainly made me feel like I was dying inside. Here's a snippet from a journal entry on I wrote on April 28th, 2015:

What do you do when you discover that you no longer desire to say all that you had to say before or when you need creativity to articulate what you're experiencing but you lack the ability? I'm venturing into a new season, and I have absolutely no idea how to navigate it all. I've fallen in love with one of the most creative people I've ever met. He's truly gifted by God in song and music. If he's a mirror, I couldn't catch up in a million years. I feel like I have nothing to give him that he doesn't already have.

I'm so broken by all of this pouring out. It's like I've given so much that there's nothing left of me. I don't know who I am. I'm no poet. No writer. No expert. No activist. Nothing. I'm a child of God. That's all I know. I wasn't born a sex-trafficking survivor, and yet that title has consumed my world. Just as CEO of Bridget's Dream has. I allowed myself to be consumed, I guess. Yet I'm frustrated. Primarily because I didn't have the opportunity to discover anything that I love doing. What do I LOVE to do? What's important to me?

I don't even know what I want to write about. I thought it was an autobiography, but I'm so tired of living in that space in my head and my life. You've reduced me to nothing, Lord. I'm not recognizable. Show me. Show me what to write, what to focus on, how to be. I don't know what I have to say. I need a revolution, a transformation. One that transcends far beyond the space I occupy today. I need brain surgery. All I do is survive. What does it even mean to thrive at this point?

Will you grant me a sabbatical; an actual time of rest? One where I'm cared for?

I'm afraid. But I don't want to be. I finally want You more than anything else. Once more.

I'd come to the end of myself and was begging God for rest. After a month and a half long sabbatical (which was really no sabbatical at all), I realized that I needed to resign from my position with Bridget's Dream, and the board eventually decided to dissolve the organization. But something else was happening. Despite the challenges and the painful lessons, I began to see that I was going deeper so that God could take me higher.

While you're on your dream journey, you'll have to go deeper so that God can take you higher. You'll have to fully embrace the pain that often precedes the promise.

When I wrote that journal entry, I saw myself as inferior to another human being, and I ended up getting my heart broken. The costly and painful result was a correction in my vision of *myself*.

When you have the correct vision of yourself *and* God you will embody the true version of yourself and experience the deepest satisfaction possible on this side of eternity.

My boyfriend turned out to be a walking contradiction. He was not who the world thought he was. But then again, neither was I, and God wanted me to see my faults in the situation so that I could understand that I was in no position to judge or refuse to forgive him. The truth is, both he *and* I were not who we displayed ourselves to be, and we were both more than the world had even begun to see of us. I finally understood what it meant to be a Christian leader with sick secrets; to live behind an image and lose myself in the process. I could no longer stand in judgment of the older generation of Christian leaders that I had once been disappointed by.

When I started Bridget's Dream, it was during a time that I had been deeply wounded at a church I was attending. I was angry with my leaders and confused; that is until I learned more about my own human propensities. Learning the truth about myself, gaining a deeper understanding of forgiveness and love, and knowing God better were priorities set for me by a loving Father. Becoming a CEO and an activist while developing "type A" tendencies were the perfect set of circumstances to mask some of my longstanding heart issues. So God removed the source of my hiding and self-deception. He gave me incredible opportunities to fulfill the desires of my heart and then when the time came to evolve, He provided me a cocoon and reminded me that being a caterpillar forever simply wasn't His best for me. I envisioned myself fighting human trafficking for my lifetime. God knew that 18 years was more than enough. My battle against human trafficking didn't begin when I started Bridget's Dream, no, it began when I was first exploited at 14. I didn't understand that He was trying to liberate me so I fought God in the process, I gradually rediscovered that His plan was better (and a whole lot less stressful) when I humble myself and surrender to it.

Who you really are is not who you display for the world to see but it's the person God sees when He's the only One that can see you. He is determined to water the dry parts of your life and mend the parts that are still broken.

This painful discovery took me on an adventure to the place where my deepest pain lived, just like my Dream Adviser Coach TJ had told me back in 2013. I finally saw what I was running from. I was running from ME! I had to go back to the Leah who disappeared from class because she felt unwanted and unloved. Back to the Leah who hid in her room when her parents would fight. Back to the Leah who concluded that no one would care if she ran away from home because she had no worth. Back to the Leah who rode her bike on a dirt path and talked to God when no one else would listen or understand.

Falling apart helped me to find ME again.
But most importantly, I found HIM!

There were many people I was able to help but it was time to hold my own hand. My painful process gave me the desire to fight for *my* dreams (not just the dreams of others), to truly love myself (I didn't know how), and to grab God's hand with my other hand. Crying agonizing tears, I walked (and sometimes crawled) with Him out of my in-between place into a brand new dream and a brand new me.

Dreams do come to an end sometimes, but only so God can give you something better and every inch of ground you covered will help to lay a foundation of victory for those coming behind you. During this season, I began to reflect on something God helped me to see. It was an incredible reminder of His plan for me and this beautiful planet He created. Here's what I reflected on:

March 3rd, 1984 was the day Bridget was born.

March 3rd, 2002 was the date Jesus saved me from the painful world of commercial sexual exploitation.

March 3rd, 2006 was, sadly, also the day that Bridget was killed.

Life, death, and a resurrected life all represented on one date in my calendar. I'd agonized over the loss of Bridget and couldn't make sense of it. I was angry for years and then, by God's grace was able to start an organization in her memory. It was painful but I had to embrace that Bridget's Dream was a season of my life and not the final chapter. It was the perfect reminder of God's plan. Death is scary; in fact, that's an understatement. As someone who knows the Giver of life personally, I understand now that I need not fear death of any sort. That liberation is available to you too. We have all been born into the greatest story ever told. Jesus already laid down His life for us. Because He died, death no longer has power over those who love Him. When we receive His gift for us, we are born again and the old version of us dies with Him. Then and only then can we experience real life on this planet for the whole world to see.

My experience with losing Bridget's Dream and being forced to face myself helped me to see my need for the Gospel all over again. My pastor, Scott Hagan of Real Life Church, taught me that believers experience a second salvation when they become leaders. And that was the case for me. I lost myself in my dream to find HIM and receive the dream that He had for me; a dream that liberates me to be what I've always wanted, even before Bridget's death. My deepest desire was for the world to know the Love of God and His power. And what better way to do that than to use *every* gift He's given me (especially my gift to write). He has generously gifted me beyond what I could once comprehend. He's done the same for you.

Your dream is not designed to run your life; you are

designed to live fully present, fully joyful, and fully satisfied as you honor the One who gave you the dream. Sure, you will have opposition. "I have told you all this so that you may have peace in me. Here on earth you will have many trials and sorrows, but take heart because I (Jesus) have overcome the world" (John 16:33 NLT). Jesus knew that every dreamer would face obstacles that can only be overcome by a mountain moving God who moves by mountain moving faith. When I started on my journey, I *did not* have mountain moving faith. I was great at proclaiming faith but something in my heart was eroding due to disappointments and unchecked bitterness. Pursuing my dream forced me to see who I really was, the good, the bad, and the ugly.

Believing I was inferior and doubting God's promises for my life were my Achilles heel. The enemy knew that and while I didn't want anyone to know that I was struggling, my life was making a liar out of me. My Dad had warned me of the possibility of living a lie when I was 18. His words of wisdom were true! When I had reached the end of my rope, my image crumbled and revealed all the problems that I had desperately been trying to conceal. Thankfully, God covered me and did not allow the world to see just how bad it got. He gave me the choice to reveal it or conceal it, and because I know that we overcome by the blood of the Lamb and the word of our testimony, my testimony is once again on display for the world to see. Unashamed.

People were looking at the "image" I let them see and concluded that I was dynamic, successful, beautiful, and many other things that I did not believe about myself. Nothing was ever enough until my heart returned to my first Love: Jesus, the best lover of my soul. All of my accomplishments were things that I thought would fulfill me. I finally had the opportunity to make use of the most painful parts of my life, yet I was pushing myself so hard that I almost had a nervous breakdown. It didn't take long for my organization to take on the shape of its leader.

Are you ready for your dream to look like you?

Well, my dream looked pretty on the outside, but on the inside it was chaotic: debt and money issues, stressed out staff members, a loss of hope and vision, confusion about what to do next, and the list goes on. By the time others became aware of it, I was on the verge of losing my mind literally. I had a total breakdown. It was a devastating time for me and I could not see my way out. For a while at least.

Around that time, my life coach, Anne Denmark of Life Discovery Coaching, sent me a gift card to Barnes & Noble as a "thank you" for a referral. Anyone who knows me knows that I love to read and that I'm a book-hoarder. I quickly made my way to the bookstore thinking I may find a book that would help me navigate this season of my life. I looked in the Christian Life section, the Business section, and in the Reference section, hoping to find something that would help me get my passion back and gain some clarity. Sitting on the aisle floor in my sweats and a coffee-stained hoodie with my hair unkempt, I called my friend, hoping that she would have a book recommendation. We began to talk, and I vented my frustrations, only to revisit the truest desires of my heart: I wanted to be an authro and I needed help figuring out the next steps of my life.

At that time I had $24 in my bank account, my business was bankrupt and ready for dissolution, my relationship with my boyfriend had ended, and I had turned down a $30,000 contract for 15 days of training because I simply couldn't handle talking about human trafficking anymore (yeah, it was that bad). Oh, and my rent was 10 days overdue.

I needed my dream to end so that a new one could emerge.

Later that day my best friend and I were at a Christian bookstore searching the isles in order to locate something that would help me. There were some books that seemed to apply, but none captured what I was going through. Toni Morrison, an incredible American novelist, once said, "If there's a book that you want to read and it hasn't been written yet, then you must write it." Those words pierced me the first time I heard them and still ring true today.

There were things I'd faced without the use of a map, but I *wished* there was a book I could turn to or someone who would understand. Add to that the fact that I'd been a frustrated writer for years. I first knew that I wanted to write a book at the age of 18, but having so many ideas and even more fears led to procrastination. The debilitating fear of not accomplishing the truest dreams in my heart fueled my avoidance and my doubts. Past pains and losses screamed louder than even my purest desires. There was a deep longing to become an original work of art. I had no desire to be what I'd seen in church. I had no desire to be what I saw in the human trafficking movement. When the confusion cleared, I found myself declaring: "I just want to be LEAH." I was in a battle between becoming who I knew that I was and staying trapped in dated versions of myself.

When we get low on our dream path and our hearts are affected by various challenges, we are most vulnerable. Vulnerability was always a source of despondency because I equated it with weakness, and weak people get hurt. Accepting myself and knowing how to navigate the new world that I found myself in seemed impossible. When I watched Bridget's Dream on the brink of dissolution, I was dying inside and I faced an identity crisis. My every prediction about my future was negative, and I began to fear that I was becoming like some of the people I'd seen growing up: hopeless and addicted, with aborted dreams. I was afraid to let anyone know what I was going through for fear that they would judge me, get annoyed with my depression, or worse yet, that they wouldn't understand and add to my affliction by giving useless advice. Sharing my experiences meant that people would see that the real "me" was not always the strong charismatic image that I hid behind. Yes, some of those characteristics were mine. Yes, I'm a great speaker and am possess the ability to inspire on stage, but once I would walk off of the stage, I would live in darkness and struggle with pessimism, discontentment, and anxiety. That was not the life that God had in mind for me.

I already knew that religion wasn't the answer. Religion had caught my attention, but it couldn't captivate or sustain me. I knew why the world was turning from traditional religious views. People were disenchanted. So was I. People thought God wasn't real. Based upon my actions and thought patterns, I didn't think God was really who the Bible claimed He was. After all, if He was who He said He was, then why was my constant uphill battle so different from other people's?

Somewhere in that process I screamed at God in prayer. I literally asked Him what the f*** He wanted from me. I was full of rage and questions. My rage seethed every time I spoke to people who cared about me but didn't understand the darkness I was facing. It often felt like I was being counseled by Job's friends so I went into isolation and avoided deep conversations about my agonies. Job's friends could not discern what God was preparing him for as he was going through immense suffering and did not have a full concept of how God moved in situations like his (if you are going through an intense time of suffering and haven't read the book of Job in the Bible yet, read it, it'll change your life). My heart turned to the Holy Scriptures for direction, once again, because of that very reason. I always loved the Bible but lost so much hope and confidence in the Truth and its supernatural role in transforming my thoughts. Having nowhere to turn for answers redirected my gaze onto the Word of Life.

It was in that place of complete confusion and uncertainty that giving up became the best option. Everything that wasn't working had to come to an end and letting myself fall into all of the things that I was trying to run from was painful but it was necessary. I plunged head first into the unknown; hoping that I would be caught and cared for. If the God of the Bible was real, He was going to have to show me.

Again.

I had met Him back in 2002, the day after the last night a trafficker ever exploited me, but I needed to encounter Him again in a fresh, new way. I didn't just need healing; I needed a new life, a new me, and a new dream. So, dreamer, the answer to the question that this chapter title poses is "no". Dreams don't die, but sometimes they end. And when they end it is because they need to. As the old song by Kenny Rogers says, "You gotta know when to hold em, know when to fold em, know when to walk away, know when to run." That song *The Gambler* was life advice being given by a card shark. Let God help you play the hand you've been dealt in a way that leads to conquest.

Sometimes the only way for us to manifest vision and leave the legacy GOD intends for us to leave is for OUR version of our dream to end.

Only God knows what's most important and what's best for His dreamers. He's the author and finisher of your faith. He's writing your story, and because of that, you can fully submit your life to Him by faith, knowing that the hope He gives does not disappoint. He's only begun to show you His goodness!

When one dream ends, a new dream will emerge and we can each spend our lives dreaming BIG dreams that God wants to bless. His first goal, however, is for the dreamer to know HIM! He invites us to a lifestyle of COMPLETE FREEDOM, MIRACLES, and BIG DREAMS. When you know Him (for real) and fall deeply in love with Him (again or perhaps for the first time), there'll be no stopping you.

VISION QUESTIONS

What needs to die/end in your life in order for you to become the truest version of yourself?

_____

_____

_____

Have you ever faced the end of a dream? If so, how could that be affecting your perspective today?

_____

_____

_____

What are some of the unhealthy ways that you cope with stressful periods? How can you avoid them as you pursue your dreams?

_____

_____

_____

God is saying to you, "Behold, I do a new thing." Everything God does is new, and He wants to do the unimaginable in your life. Whether you believe it fully or not, He _wants_ to exceed your expectations. It will not be easy, but it will be easiest when your heart fully trusts that He is real and that He is a rewarder of all those who diligently seek Him. How would your perspective of your life change if you embraced this truth? What are you hoping God will do with you and your legacy?

_____

_____

_____

_____

YOU ARE THE DREAM...

I grabbed her soft wrinkled hand, rubbing my fingers across her blue and yellow diamond ring, the one I'd always admired from the time I was just a little girl.

"Mommiesmoms, did you ever have a dream you didn't fulfill; something you really wanted but never pursued?"

She looked at me and then glanced off into the distance. "Sure I did. When I was in high school…"

High school? Was my grandmother seriously telling me that there was a dream all the way from back in high school that she had and didn't fulfill? My heart was heavy as I looked at her, realizing that she was 85 years old and had never fulfilled her dream. Nearly seven decades were behind her as she looked back on the days of her youth.

"You know that section of your high school year book that has pictures of certain students with a title that says 'Most Likely to Become'?"

I nodded my head yes.

"Well, my classmates put my picture in there and said that I was most likely to become a playwright or poet."

I was amazed as I gazed at this beautiful woman. The woman who sang me the song "When I grow too old to dream, I'll have you to remember. When I grow too old to dream, your kiss will live in my heart."

That woman. She never got to experience the fulfillment of her dream.

Or did she?

CHAPTER EIGHT
You Are the Dream!

I was so deeply impacted by that conversation with my Mommiesmoms (my Grandmother) that I decided to ask my dad and my mom the same question. I discovered that as a young man, my dad had wanted to go to the Olympics and to be a model. I had no clue. My mom had always wanted to be a musician but also felt that part of that dream was because she was trying to win her father's approval, as my grandfather, Franklin Love Albright, had been a saxophonist for Frank Sinatra and Elvis. So at 53, my mom still wasn't quite sure what her dream was. I was astonished. Never did I think to ask the people that had raised me what their dreams were.

Earlier that year my Mommiesmoms had moved to Sacramento to be closer to me and my mother. We're a funny bunch. There are only three of us. All only children, and all women who've shared such similar yet vastly different struggles. So it was interesting when after years of living in separate cities we were all suddenly living in the same one. Around that time Mommiesmoms got sick and ended up in the hospital for a few days. My mom was out of town for work, so I ended up picking Mommiesmoms up from the hospital when she was released.

That night we went to her new apartment, and when she had gotten settled on the bed, my phone rang. It was the hospital calling to tell us that the IV needle was still in her arm. Unbelievable. Sure enough, it was. So they talked me through removing it. As I looked at my grandmother's delicate skin and fragile state, I was overcome with emotion. I slowly pulled the needle out and placed a cotton ball with some medical tape over it right before she collapsed into my arms. Sobbing, she whispered a statement in my ear that I will never forget.

"Leah, you are the fulfillment of my hopes and all of my dreams."

Wow! Me? The one whose organization was falling apart. Me? The one who was making a mess of her life. Me? The one who battled unending thoughts of inadequacy. Yes, she was talking about ME.

And now I want to talk about you! This book is about YOU.

What you need to understand is that you were a dream in someone's heart long before you could accomplish a single solitary thing. What matters most is that **you are God's dream**, and He has a plan for you that only HE can produce. Your striving, ingenuity, ability, and passions are secondary to Him, and sometimes, quite frankly, they won't matter at all because in the end He is more powerful than you and that's a good thing. There is

ONE who knows you best, and He knows HOW to bless you and use your life in a way that only He can. He knows when you've had all you can take and He promises you rest, even if He has to *make* you rest.

The second thing I want you to consider is that you may be the fulfillment of someone else's dream, you may be a part of someone else's legacy, or your children or children's children may be *your* legacy. Whether they are your biological children or children God blessed you to parent; they may be the manifestation of your vision. You may already be living your legacy.

Remember, a BIG dream is not about size... it's about significance.

I learned that the old proverb "Grandchildren are the crown of grandparents" is true (Proverbs 17:6). Until the day that I sat on my grandmother's porch, holding her hand and talking about dreams, I hadn't realized that she'd given me such a significant gift towards my future dream. I thought that I had no passions or dreams about specific things as a child, but at eight years old she had me reading Maya Angelou, at ten Edgar Alan Poe, and libraries were my favorite place both she and my mother would take me. Literature, books, and writing were a major theme in my life.

One of my fondest memories is of sitting on my bed in Germany one night when Mommiesmoms flew across the great waters to visit us in Europe when I was seven. My mother and Mommiesmoms were in my room before I went to bed, and they asked me to read them poetry. My little mind couldn't fully grasp the depth of what I was reading, so I was perplexed when I looked up and saw them both crying. I hope that I can do that again when the two of them read these words.

Mom and Mommiesmoms, thank you for giving me the gift of reading and writing. Mom, thank you for starting to read to me when I was 18 months. I'm sure your heart was filled with joy when at four years old I began reading to you. Bet you never thought that gift you gave me would turn into a book you could hold in your hands, huh? Mommiesmoms, your dream didn't die; it grew up! And it became a woman named Leah Jonet Albright-Byrd who is now a published author. I love you too much my OAO. I pray both of you can forgive me for all of my distance over the last some years. God was helping me discover HIS dream for me, and now I'm living it. And to all my readers, you are much more important than any dream you can conceive.

You are the apple of God's eye, His prize possession, His dream manifested. You are God's legacy. There's no greater dream than the one you see when you look in the mirror.

You can put your plans on paper and prepare your path, "but the Lord's purposes will prevail" (Proverbs 19:21). God's dream for every dreamer is to see Him more clearly and to follow Him more nearly. He is your Prince of Peace, your Great Physician, and the Master of all things.

Nothing in this world can take the place of a relationship with the Holy One. Have you been restricting Him to the limits of your human logic? Or perceiving Him through the lens of cultural distortions and bad experiences? A prideful heart believes it knows all there is to know about spirituality and God. It's okay to be angry and even turned off but I don't want you to be turned away. I am not speaking of Christianity as a religious construct. There are those of you that will think of Christ and church and be repelled because of wicked things that other people have done. But you can't allow other people's mistakes and misinterpretations of God to destroy your opportunity to know Him. God's enemy has blinded the hearts of so many people; people who God loves dearly but whose free will He will not override. Christianity is not a religion, it is the way to the Father. If you are not a believer, all I ask is that you open your mouth and say "God, reveal yourself to me! I don't know all there is to know and I'm not certain of who You are but I want to know the truth! I don't want to run the risk of being so set in what I think I know that I miss you."

If you are someone who already knows Christ, you must never allow your dreams to become more important to you than the One who gave you your life and everything you need in order to see those dreams come to fruition. You are not defined by your dream because *you are the dream*. He's just waiting for you to understand that.

Will you let Him take you deeper and higher?

I'll be honest, to most dreamers it will probably appear that you're not going anywhere in this season. But the keyword there is "appear". When my dream ended, my life came to a complete standstill. The hustle and bustle I lived in as a CEO and activist ceased and I faced four major dream lessons:

1. *when a dream ends, you must celebrate your progress and avoid the temptation to fixate on your mistakes*

2.   *you must learn how valuable YOU are apart from what you DO*

3.   *God can take a season of painful toil and turn it into a season of restful production*

4.   *holding onto your version of your dream can make your season of transition more painful and reveal the biggest human obstacle: trusting God. I didn't trust my truest Friend. Don't be like me.*

Our culture prides itself in constant busyness. Yet our best efforts can never produce the success we'll experience when we realize that being a dreamer is not about our version of success. All of my effort to build Bridget's Dream, my striving, and stress, my doubts and my fears, did not produce the fruit that I longed for. He wanted me to learn how to rest in Him and inherit promises that I did not have to fight to earn. Don't believe the lie that your value lies in your ability to produce. Believing the American concept of success can dominate your life and prevent you from experiencing God's version of success. I'll give one of the best examples I've ever seen.

"One day as Jesus was standing by the Lake of Gennesaret, the people were crowding around him and listening to the word of God. He saw at the water's edge two boats, left there by the fishermen, who were washing their nets. He got into one of the boats, the one belonging to Simon, and asked him to put out a little from shore. Then he sat down and taught the people from the boat. When he had finished speaking, he said to Simon, "Put out into deep water, and let down the nets for a catch."

Simon answered, "Master, we've worked hard all night and haven't caught anything. But because you say so, I will let down the nets." When they had done so, they caught such a large number of fish that their nets began to break. So they signaled their partners in the other boat to come and help them, and they came and filled both boats so full that they began to sink.

When Simon Peter saw this, he fell at Jesus' knees and said, "Go away from me, Lord; I am a sinful man!" For he and all his companions were astonished at the catch of fish they had taken, and so were James and John, the sons of Zebedee, Simon's partners."(Luke 5:1-10, NIV).

What Simon Peter and his business partners experienced was frustrating. They had spent their energy and effort toiling and were unable to produce their desired goal; even though they were skilled fisherman. Being a dreamer is not about ability, it's about humility. Jesus stepped in and gave them instruction. They obeyed despite their experience and professional expertise and they were able to accomplish (in a moment) what they'd spent an entire night attempting to do. This example isn't just about our toil and His instruction. It's about the shift that comes when God interrupts our efforts and redirects our focus. Jesus divinely interrupted their best efforts for a greater purpose. Notice Peter's response. When he obeyed and saw the result, you'd think he'd respond rejoicing only about the sudden success he experienced. Instead his focus was shifted off of the task at hand and onto what Jesus wanted him to see. He obeyed, by faith, and responded with an acknowledgement of who he was "Go away from me Lord, I am a sinful man." He suddenly saw himself and became keenly aware of his imperfection with a deep sense of unworthiness.

But listen to the response of His friend Jesus.

Jesus simply responded: "Do not be afraid, from now on you will fish for people." And that is what He's saying to all of us dreamers. Do not be afraid. Do not fear your inabilities. Do not fear your past mistakes. Do not be afraid of anything. Your dream journey is about coming face-to-face with yourself and your Maker, embracing your bright and dark side, and trusting in the One who has a vision for your life that is far greater than you can imagine. He wants to use your experiences (both the successes and failures) to partner with you in the fulfillment of *His* dream for your life: to be a FISHER OF PEOPLE. He wants all of the world to know Him and you get to join Him on that journey.

So I ask you again:

Will you let Him take you deeper and higher? Will you surrender EVERYTHING so that you can follow Him on His dream journey for this world?

VISION QUESTIONS

What are the BIG dreams of three of your closest friends/family members? Do you know? Sometimes we go through life without realizing the treasure buried in the people right in front of us. If you don't know and want to be inspired, I encourage you to go ask them and write their answers here.

_____

_____

_____

_____

If you have parented others or are a grandparent now, how are your children/grandchildren a manifestation of your dream/vision? What seeds can you sow into them now that will teach them to dream and manifest their own visions some day?

_____

_____

_____

_____

Knowing that you are God's dream is powerful, and as His dream, it is important for you to know that He died so that you can REST IN HIM and cast the burden of your dream upon Him. What did God reveal to you in this chapter?

_____

_____

_____

_____

EVERYTHING AND NOTHING...

"Leah, can I read this to you?"

I looked at my friend Nate's fiancée and saw in her so much of what I saw in myself. God had brought me hundreds of miles across the country to a place of sanctuary with a girl who shared my name. Leah had opened up her house and her heart and gave me a refuge; a place like my old dirt path, where I could daydream about the future. The place where I wrote the bulk of this book.

"Sure you can read to me, Leah!" She sat down, placed her puppy Chica on her lap, and looked at me with eager expectation.

Together we sat and listened to the words of a famous Christian author in one of her books. Both of us Leahs knew what it was like to get trapped in cycles that kept us from moving forward with our dreams, and we were both realizing that the only way we'd make it in the next phase of our lives was to undergo a significant change.

CONCLUSION
Everything and Nothing

Surrendering my dream to Jesus was, to date, one of the hardest times of obedience and submission I've encountered. Learning to trust that following Him and being His dream is far greater than anything I could envision for my life has certainly not been an easy journey. Particularly for someone who learned to distrust others very early on. One of my core inner beliefs was that it wasn't okay for me to need anyone and when I became a Christian and experienced serious betrayals from other believers, unanswered/delayed prayers, and a host of other disappointments, that lie was reinforced. Believing, truly believing, that He is all I need and all I truly desire has been surprisingly painful. When I was stripped of everything I defined myself by, I saw my true self and I saw Him more clearly than ever before. Clearly I cannot say that my process was simple. It came with infuriating pains and wounds that left scars. But what was most painful was when I began to believe lies about Him and His promises. Now I know that becoming a butterfly and living my dreams was about the imago phase of the lifecycle. In Latin, the words imago dei, mean image of God. We were created in the image of God. The fall of man warped that image and the Son of Man fixed that image. Can we be without sin? Not entirely. Not until this world comes to an end. But, we can be filled to overflowing with supernatural love, power, and dreams.

"I am the vine; you are the branches. If you remain in me and I in you, you will bear much fruit; apart from me you can do nothing." John 15:5, NIV

The hardest and the best part of being on the path of the dreamer is the discovery that our lives are an interesting paradox of realities.

We are both nothing at all and everything at the same time! When I came to Jesus, I could not hold my head high and I saw myself as worthless. My accusers stood around me, ready to hurt me with their judgments just like the woman caught in adultery (see John 8:1-11). I came into the Kingdom of God the lowest way any person in this world can come. To the world I was a prostitute; someone shunned by society and frequently harshly judged.

The walk of shame I once took after a long night on the streets of San Francisco back in 1999, was a chilling taunt from the father of lies (satan). I had to walk a few miles to a dark cold hotel room at 6am, when people were just on their way to work. My feet were burning, I was 15 years old, and was as lost as lost can be. With no jacket, the chill burned through my bones so I walked into a gas station to get something warm to drink. I dared not look anyone in the eyes for fear of the disgust and judgment that I'd surely see. Their stares were piercing; people who thought I was nothing and felt that they were superior to me were commonplace in my world back then. Today, that memory has lost all of its sting. Just like God promised me.

It seemed like a dream, too good to be true,
when GOD returned Zion's exiles. We laughed, we sang,
we couldn't believe our good fortune. We were the talk
of the nations, "GOD was wonderful to them!"
GOD was wonderful to us; we are one happy people.
And now, GOD, do it again – bring rains to our drought-
stricken lives, so those who planted their crops in despair
will shout hurrahs at the harvest, so those who went off
with heavy hearts will come home laughing, with
armloads of blessing. (Psalm 126 MSG)

In the beginning of this book, I shared some dialogue I had with a Dream Adviser who asked me the question "Do you know why that makes you angry?" He asked me that in response to a statement that I told him was commonly said about people who shared my history. They were often told that they would always be stuck in the state that they were in. They were brainwashed into believing that they were permanently flawed. But you don't have to share my experiences to be brainwashed into believing things that aren't true about yourself and your dreams. That's why it's important for *all of us* to remember one of the first truths I shared when you joined me on this journey.

The number one obstacle for any dreamer is DECEPTION.

Deception made me so angry that I became determined to dream. I used my anger for something positive, until it was time for me to be completely transformed so that God could give me a new dream.

One night, back in 2001, Bridget and I hopped in the car at 2am after a pimp accused me of being incapable of pursuing my dream of going to college. I was determined to prove that I was capable of more than anyone had even begun to see. By March 3rd, 2002, I was so desperate for help that I wanted either freedom or death. I was willing to die to be free. But I didn't realize that someone already did that for me until I stood face-to-face with the force of true LOVE. I needed a Savior. And when I despaired of life itself, He stepped in and gave me a dream. I quickly saw that I was nothing without HIM and was overcome with gratitude that He actually loved me as I was (when society rejected me and I felt that no one truly loved me). When the world seemed to hate me, I found my refuge in His arms, and I've been there ever since.

That's the condition of every human being in this world. We are nothing without Him. Even the gifts we have are gifts that *He* gave to us.

It is only pride and the voice of God's enemy (satan) who will aim to convince us that we are sufficient without our Creator. Truth is not ours for the choosing. Truth is a Person. When Jesus was facing His own crucifixion, "Pilate said, 'So you are a king?' Jesus responded, 'You say I am a king. Actually, I was born and came into the world to testify to the truth. All who love the truth recognize that what I say is true.' 'What is truth?' Pilate asked. (John 18:37-38, NLT). Isn't that the question of our day? Isn't that what lingers in the back of our minds as we watch the latest global affairs and tragedies unfold. What is truth? Truth is a Person. "I am the way, the truth, and the life. No one can come to the Father except through me." (John 14:6, NLT). This is not about a religion. It's about a person. Jesus, son of God and son of man, by His death, gave us all access to the One we long for: our Heavenly Father.

By that sacrifice and my acceptance of the gift of salvation, I now know the Source of the best love there is; a love that snatched an 18 year old girl from the gates of hell and turned her whole life around; a love that turned the tragic murder of Bridget Gray into an organization that shook up my whole community and changed the world forever; a love that saw that I needed a deeper healing than I could fathom and snatched me out of my own destructive cycle to give me a brand new dream and a brand new life.

When I first encountered Christ it was much easier to accept that I was nothing without Him and everything with Him because I saw myself as lowly. Lowly, however, turned into worthlessness and perfectionism rooted in performance because of the deception. I felt I was inadequate to bring money into my organization, worried excessively about my appearance as a leader, and questioned my abilities. All of those misperceptions about myself were strikingly similar to the lies the enemy tried to convince me of when I was being prostituted as a child. He tried to convince me once again that my value was in money, appearance, and performance. And with that in mind, look at the parallels of those lies and the lies we all believe as Americans. A spirit of prostitution rests over this great Nation and now I see that my calling is greater than fighting human trafficking. My call is to fight the enslavement found in America through the lies I've mentioned. My call is to this great Nation and all of its brokenness. The solution is found in LOVE, sweet LOVE, and I know Him and the American struggle very intimately. As life and my weaknesses would have it, I stopped believing in Love for a while. I was jaded from all of my pain and doubted God's goodness. He allowed me to rebel, to walk away, and to question His heart until I saw, once again, that I needed Him the most.

More than a dream, more than a vision, more than a legacy, we need JESUS.

We are nothing without Him, but we can be everything with Him. If you do not know Him and you struggle to believe that He is the Savior I'm telling you He is, it's okay to ask Him to reveal Himself to you and guide you to Himself. There are many deceptions in the world today aiming to convince us they are true, but there is a Name that is above every name and He sets captives free and gives gifts to us all.

When I was 18, a few months before I first became deeply aware that Jesus was real, I got on my knees in my room and cried saying "God, if you're real, I want to know You!" I let pride go and what I *thought* I understood and He answered that sincere request. I know He'll do the same for you.

If you already know Him, what exactly are you waiting for? It's time to dream BIGGER!

Our expectations often don't align with God's abilities. If we are honest with ourselves, sometimes we do not have the response of faith that Simon Peter had in Luke 5:1-10, who obeyed Jesus despite his own expertise and failures. Sometimes we resist Him and choose "good" over God. That's why I wrote this book for dreamers; for people who know that they were made for more. I'm not speaking as an expert but as a fellow dreamer who has seen the beauty of a dream pursued and conquered. The day I held in my hands an award from the California State

Senate celebrating my contributions to the Human Trafficking movement was surreal. Seeing the way my state and my country has evolved in its systematic response to Human Trafficking is definitely a dream come true. But none of it compares to the joy of knowing that I am following the One who created me for my unique destiny. He stripped me of titles that restricted me and made me prideful. He disciplined and healed my wayward thoughts and broken heart. He gave me an unforgettable opportunity to experience victory in an area of life that nearly destroyed mine and because He is the best Father there is He let me know, in His time, that there was so much more in store for me. And He has so much in store for YOU!

Does this book have all the answers? Of course not. Some of the answers you will just have to discover on your own path. But I'm here, if you ever need me and I do hope that you keep in touch. This journey will be tough, as it will bring out the best and the worst in you, but you will know yourself and God in ways you never imagined possible, and in the end, no matter how painful the process, it will all be worth it.

VISION QUESTIONS

What are your takeaways after reading *Determined to Dream*?

_____

_____

_____

_____

_____

_____

What's next for you on <u>your</u> dream journey?

_____

_____

_____

_____

_____

_____

These last two questions (like the rest) are for your private dream journey but if you're open to it, I'd love to hear from you and discover what you've learned and what's next for you. Leah@leahjonet.com

ABOUT THE AUTHOR

LEAH JONET ALBRIGHT-BYRD is a dreamer! She has been featured on Oprah Winfrey, Katie Couric, BET News, and Being Mary Jane. She was also the recipient of an Emmy-award after an appearance focused on educating viewers about civil rights issues and America's human trafficking epidemic.

Her media and speaking opportunities coupled with the obstacles she faced on her own dream journey reawakened a passion for reaching the masses with a much needed message of hope. Her dream of authorship could not be ignored so she returned to one of her first loves and began to write. Her deepest yearning is to see others awakened to God's love and power and what better way to do that than through the art form that God chose to make Himself known to the world.

Leah loves singing, photography, and her guitar. She's discovering how to not allow titles to restrict or define her and looks forward to each new dream God is leading her to!

Made in the USA
San Bernardino, CA
12 October 2016